PROBLEMS:SOLUTIONS
Visual Thinking for Graphic Communicators

Richard Wilde

 Van Nostrand Reinhold Company
New York

Library of Congress Catalog Card Number 86-9203

ISBN 0-442-29182-5

Printed in Hong Kong by Everbest Printing Co., Ltd.

Designed by Richard Wilde
Art direction: Richard Wilde, Russ D'Anna
Design assistant: Tom Park

Van Nostrand Reinhold Company Inc.
115 Fifth Avenue
New York, New York 10003

Van Nostrand Reinhold Company Limited
Molly Millars Lane
Wokingham, Berkshire RG11 2PY, England

Van Nostrand Reinhold
480 La Trobe Street
Melbourne, Victoria 3000, Australia

Macmillan of Canada
Division of Canada Publishing Corporation
164 Commander Boulevard
Agincourt, Ontario M1S 3C7, Canada

16 15 14 13 12 10 9 8 7 6 5 4 3 2 1

Library of Congress Cataloging-in-Publication Data

Wilde, Richard.
   Problems, solutions.

   Includes index.
   1. Visual communication—Decision-making. 2. Graphic
arts—Technique.   I. Title.
NC997.W496   1986   741.6   86-9203
ISBN 0-442-29182- 5

CONTENTS

ACKNOWLEDGMENTS

To David Rhodes for his support and encouragement.

To Marshall Arisman for his wisdom.

To Pam Manser for keeping such accurate records.

To my editors, Dorothy Spencer and Linda Venator —Dorothy for her enthusiasm and perception; Linda for her expertise and understanding.

To Dr. John Lidstone who believed in me and helped me find a publisher

To Leo Kaufman, my first real teacher, and to the others who followed: Leon Friend, Gabriel Ladderman, Jeffrey Metzner, and Dr. Josef Garai.

To Mario Gambaccini for his enthusiasm and support of student work.

To Clarence Baylis and Al Mauro for their hard work and help in coordinating student exhibitions.

Special thanks to Master Eagle Family of Companies for donating numerous color separations that help enrich the quality of the book and to Rosendahls Bogtrykkeri for also donating color separations.

To Russ D'Anna for his patience and good advice.

To Tom Park for his invaluable help and assistance in designing the book.

To Ken Ambrose for his time and experience in photographing many student projects.

To David Fishman for his expertise in photographing artwork, photo composition, and chrome retouching.

To Maurice Sherman for diligently photographing student projects.

And last, to my mother for instilling in me a capacity to save *everything,* including student artwork, which helped make this book possible.

This book is dedicated with warmest thanks and great affection to Silas H. Rhodes, cofounder, first president, and chairman of the board of the School of Visual Arts, who created the conditions that made this book possible, and to the students of the School of Visual Arts whose work appears in this book.

FOREWORD

Today's reigning debate among design educators and practicing designers concerns the balance of emphasis on design theory versus practice. Of late, design theoreticians have developed a language so obtuse that it is unintelligible to everyone except the theoreticians. This compounds the already difficult task of explaining to a student why a design solution "works" and why it doesn't. In our profession, this seems pathetically ironic when we remember that the goal of graphic design is effective communication.

Richard Wilde, chairman of the Graphic Design and Advertising departments of the School of Visual Arts, strongly emphasizes design practice as a means for students to grasp design theory. The premise is that the student learns by doing. Wilde hires a broad range of working professionals to teach both general and specialized courses. These instructors often have very different approaches to problem solving, as well as diverse teaching methods. This could become chaotic and confusing to the student, except for the guidance of Richard Wilde.

Wilde has deliberately provided a broad range of design options from which students can select. He guides them to those courses most suitable to their talents and needs. Wilde discerns the temperament and potential of each student by teaching a general graphic design course for sophomores that is required of all students, the one common thread in SVA's diverse design curriculum.

Wilde's course stresses basic graphic problem solving. Students are often presented with worksheets in which a problem is carefully stated and spaces are designated for the solution. The problems are orchestrated to enable the students to discover graphic analogies, scale relationships, ironies, color principles, and typographic solutions. By the end of the sophomore year, SVA design students have grasped the basis of a visual vocabulary on which they will draw for the rest of their careers. As the students master problem solving, they can begin to articulate the process. Hence theory follows practice.

This book is a compendium of the problems created by Richard Wilde for his students and their resulting solutions. The bulk of this work was produced on the sophomore level, and the results are impressive. Also included are more professionally accomplished pieces produced for the school exhibitions and work executed for clients, usually done by junior and senior students. These serve as a reminder to designers and educators everywhere that one solution is worth a thousand words.

Paula Scher

PREFACE

The task of all creative visual communicators is to interpret problems in a personal way while meeting the needs of other people. In the classroom, innovative problems that dictate challenging solutions help students move toward this goal.

This book consists of original visual communication problems, given at the college level, which emphasize developing a conceptual approach to problem solving. These problems encourage students to examine carefully the transition from conceptualization to execution. Emphasizing concept rather than technique gives rise to individual executions that lead to a genuine interest in developing one's craft. These problems also help to encourage students to believe in their own abilities, enabling them to function in an ever-changing society.

Problems represent opportunities that allow for growth. Solutions represent an interpretation of a problem from an individual point of view at a particular stage in one's development. This book is about PROBLEMS and SOLUTIONS

PROBLEMS:SOLUTIONS
Visual Thinking for Graphic Communicators

PART 1. DISCOVERING THE PRINCIPLES
OF VISUAL COMMUNICATION

The following assignments promote understanding of fundamental design ideas and principles, helping to lay a foundation of basic knowledge for the visual communicator. Each of these problems is concerned with a specific learning objective. In some cases the intention is made clear; in others it is not apparent, for an important part of any problem is in discerning the nature of the problem. These problems allow graphic communicators to focus on a specific aspect of graphic communication while developing their own means of solving design problems.

PROBLEM: TYPOGRAPHIC PORTRAITS

SAMPLE PROBLEM:

A specific personality is described in the twelve designated areas that appear on the assignment sheet. Visualize the character of the person described. Then, using your whole name, part of your name, or your nickname, choose an appropriate typeface for each individual personality and carefully render your name in the given area. Consider the style of the typeface, the weight of the typeface, the size of the typeface, the letter spacing, and the use of upper- and lower-case characters. Give special attention to the actual size and placement of your name in the given area.

SPECIFICATIONS

Size: As indicated on assignment sheet.
Color: Black and white. (Color should be considered only if it is integral to your concept.)
Medium: Pencil or ink.
Limitation: All solutions must be hand-lettered. Press type is unacceptable.
Suggestions: Study the typefaces found in type specimen books before making your selections. Use a luciograph to increase or decrease your type solutions to desired size.

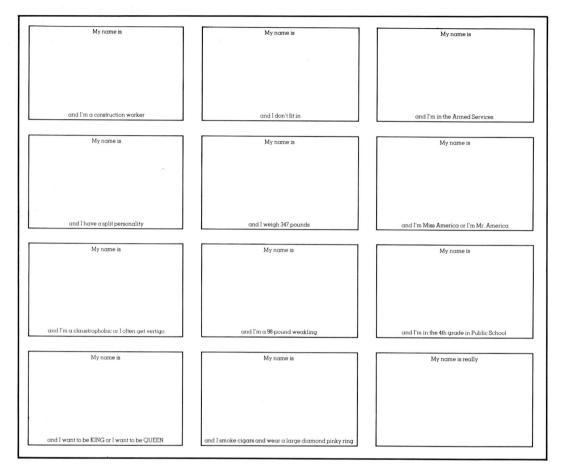

My name is
TOM
and I'm a construction worker

My name is
박 찬 문
and I don't fit in

My name is
"TOM PARK, SIR"
and I'm in the Armed Services

My name is
tho**MAS**
and I have a split personality

My name is
TOM
and I weigh 347 pounds

My name is
Thomas
and I'm Miss America or I'm Mr. America

MY NAME IS TOM AND I'M A CLAUSTRO-PHOBIC

My name is
T O M
and I'm a 98-pound weakling

My name is
TOM PARK
and I'm in the 4th grade in Public School

My name is
and I want to be KING or I want to be QUEEN

My name is
TRP
and I smoke cigars and wear a large diamond pinky ring

My name is really

Tom Park

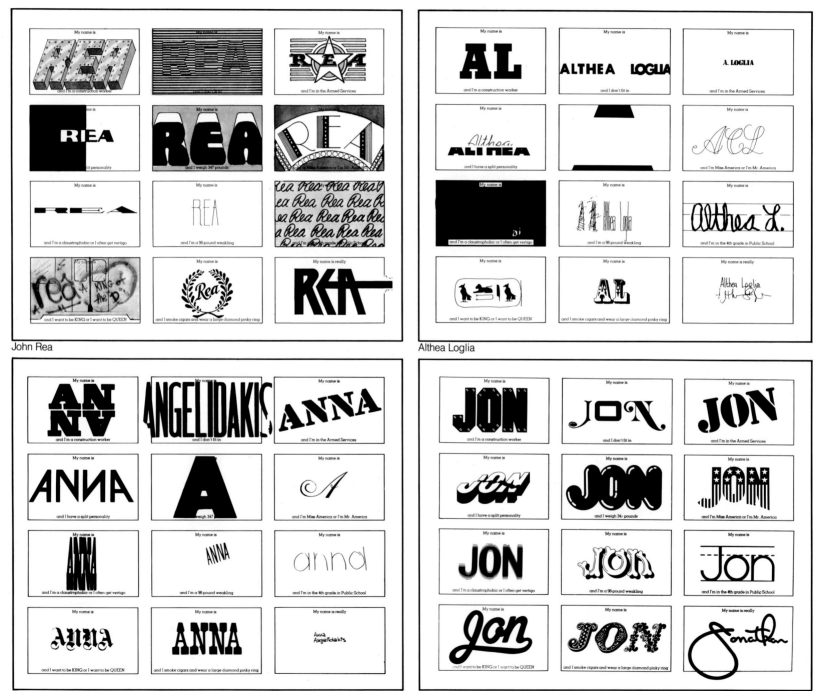

John Rea

Althea Loglia

Anna Angelidakis

Jon Volk

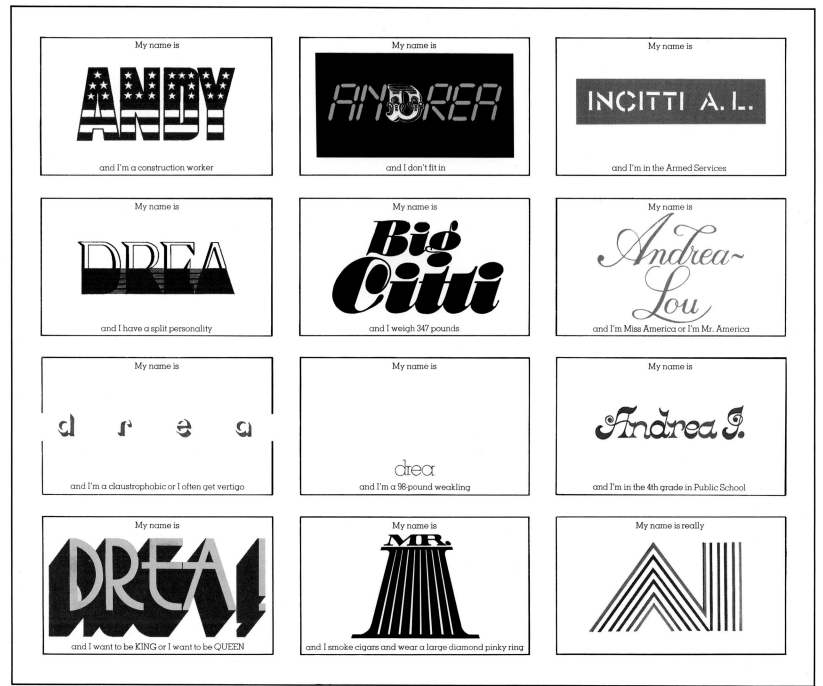

Andrea Incitti

SOLUTION:

NOTE: Although the following two solutions clearly go beyond the limitations of the problem, they are successful in their own right.

Rita Dubas

20

Kevin O'Callaghan

SOLUTION:

SOLUTION:

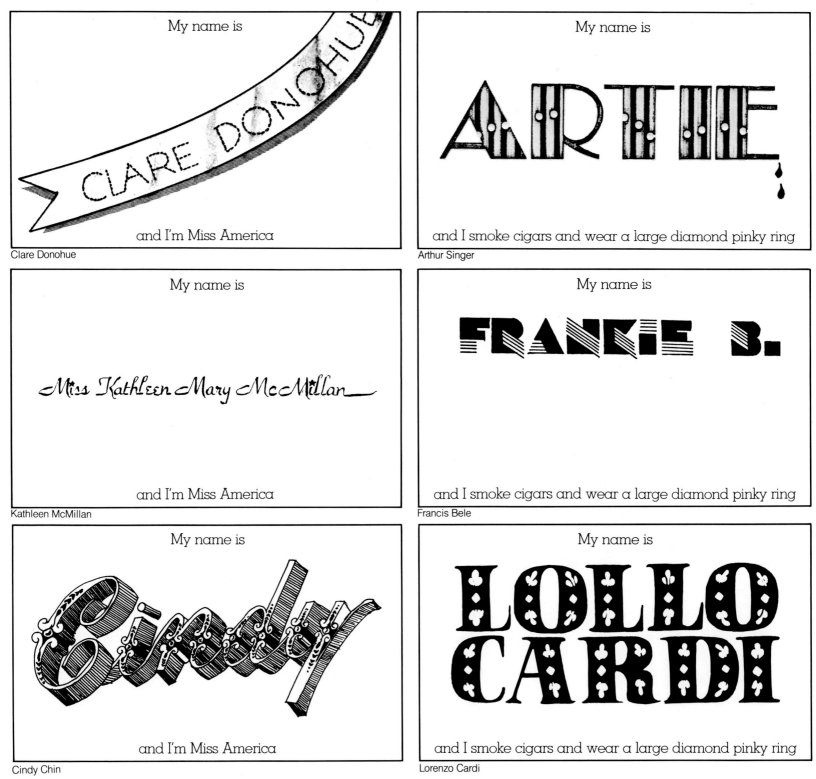

My name is

CLARE DONOHUE

and I'm Miss America

Clare Donohue

My name is

ARTIE

and I smoke cigars and wear a large diamond pinky ring

Arthur Singer

My name is

Miss Kathleen Mary McMillan

and I'm Miss America

Kathleen McMillan

My name is

FRANKIE B.

and I smoke cigars and wear a large diamond pinky ring

Francis Bele

My name is

Cindy

and I'm Miss America

Cindy Chin

My name is

LOLLO CARDI

and I smoke cigars and wear a large diamond pinky ring

Lorenzo Cardi

SOLUTION:

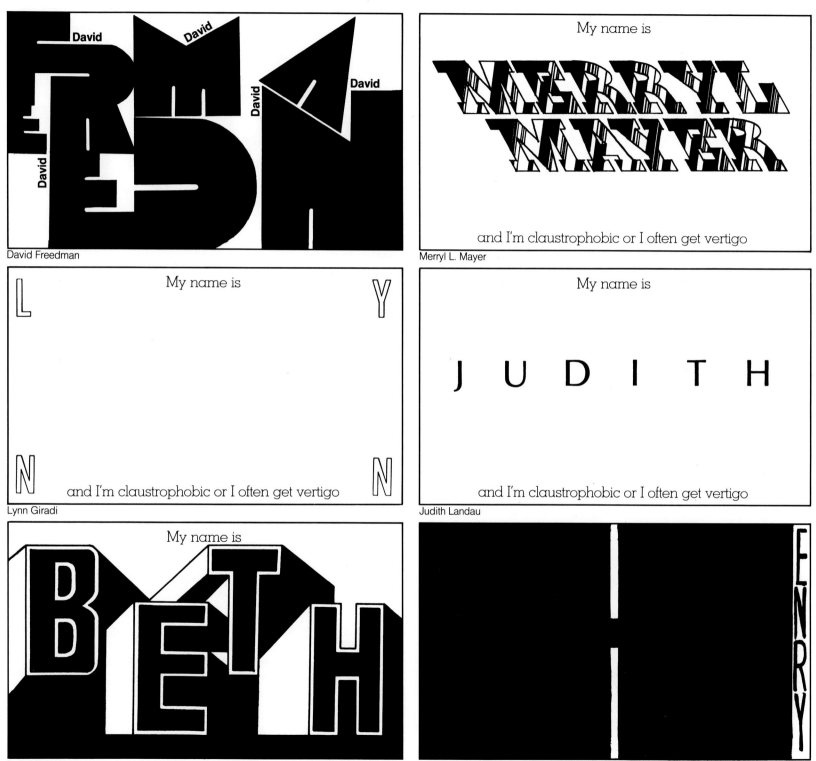

David Freedman

Merryl L. Mayer
My name is
and I'm claustrophobic or I often get vertigo

Lynn Giradi
My name is
and I'm claustrophobic or I often get vertigo

Judith Landau
My name is
JUDITH
and I'm claustrophobic or I often get vertigo

Beth Migliore
My name is

Henry Yee

SOLUTION:

My name is ... Carlos Alden ... and I don't fit in
Carlos Alden

My name is ... Stephen Silvestri ... and I don't fit in
Stephen Silvestri

My name is ... christine ... and I don't fit in
Christine Zepf

My name is ... WENDY ... and I don't fit in
Wendy Kassner

... and I don't fit in
Steven Cohn

My name is ... NONE OF YOUR @*#.!! BUSINESS! ... and I don't fit in
Clyde Henriques

SOLUTION:

My name is

J O D E E
J O D E E
J O D E E
J O D E E

and I'm in the Armed Services

Jodee Stringham

My name is

in, Gary M... missing i

and I'm in the Armed Services

Gary M. Franklin

My name is

HYO
CHA
KOO

and I'm in the Armed Services

Hyocha Koo

My name is

and I'm in the Armed Services

Christian Fencht

35687334
REGA

Christyn E. Gregan

My name is

KIRBY

and I'm in the Armed Services

Kirby Rodriguez

SOLUTION:

My name is
RON LEIGHTON
and I weigh 347 pounds

Ron Leighton

My name is
and I weigh 347 pounds

Alan Labate

My name is
and I weigh 347 pounds

Elizabeth Press

My name is
sCOTt
and I weigh 347 pounds

Scott Wadler

Abbe Eckstein

Ed Smith

SOLUTION:

John Clapps

John Clapps

Claire Mendelson

PROBLEM: ALPHABET ANALOGY

Typography is an essential element of graphic design. A designer's use of type can be as personally expressive as a painter's use of color is. Choose one character of the alphabet and redesign or reinterpret it into a personalized letterform that conveys any concept you wish. A single letter may be transformed into a visual that represents an entire concept.

SPECIFICATIONS

Size: 6½ by 6½ inches.
Color: Black and white.
Medium: No limitation.
Note: Line or tone solutions are acceptable.

SOLUTION:

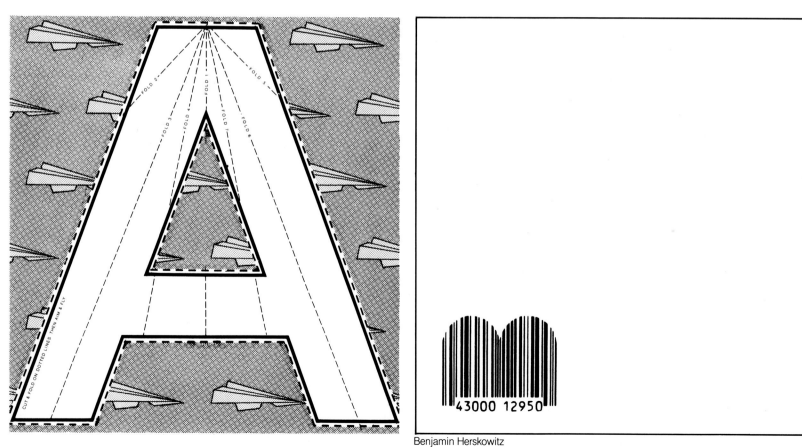

Benjamin Herskowitz

Richard Radice

James Sarfati

Glen Edelstein

Frank D'Ambrosio

Laura Goodman

Elizabeth Fischl

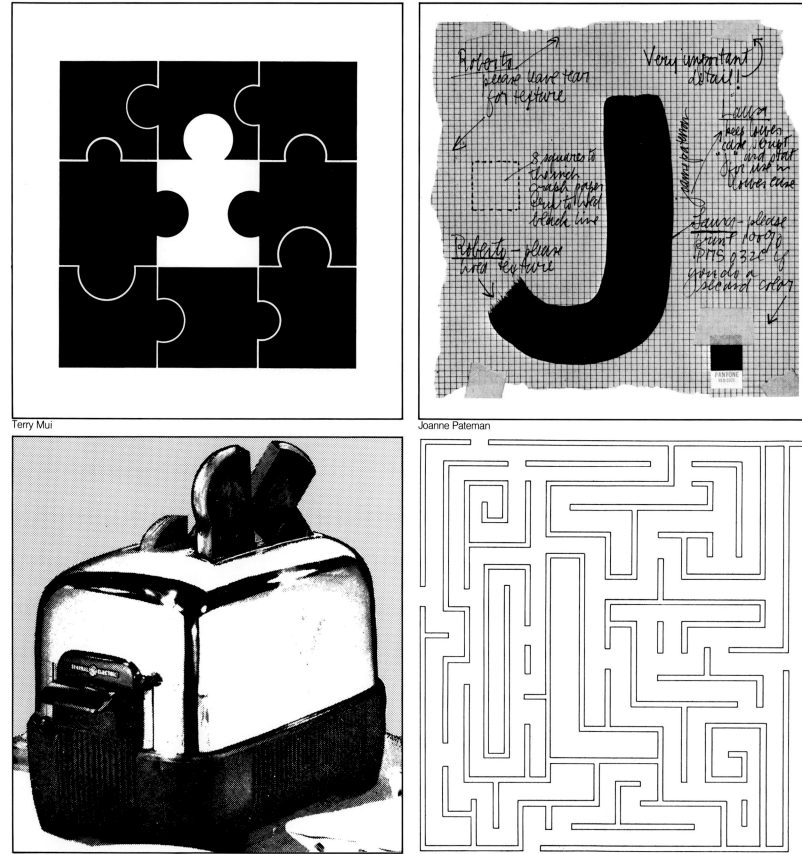

Terry Mui

Joanne Pateman

Kevin O'Callaghan

Karliese Greiner

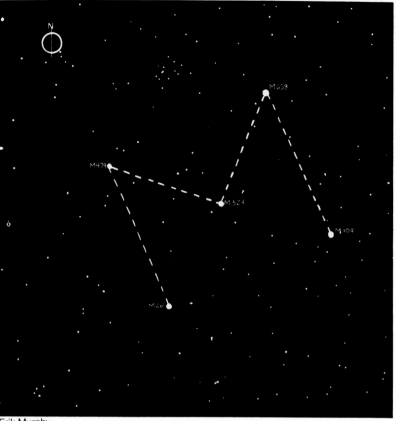

Erik Murphy

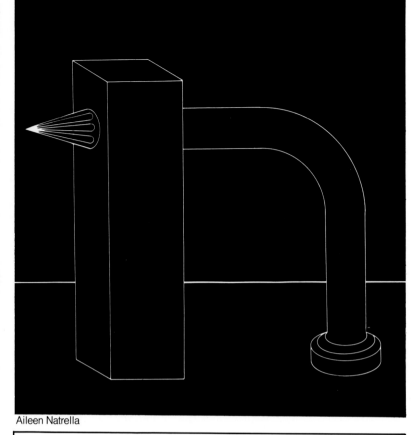

Aileen Natrella

This is dummy copy. It is not meant to be read. The purpose is to show the color and the size of this type face in the layout. This is dummy copy. It is not meant to be read. The purpose is to show the color and size of this type face in the layout. This is dummy copy. It is not meant to be read. The purpose is to show the color and size This is dummy copy. It is not meant to be read. The purpose is to show the color and the size of this type face in the layout. This is dummy copy. It is not meant to be read. The purpose is to show the color and size of this type face in the layout. This is dummy copy. It is not meant to be read. The purpose is to show the color and size This is dummy copy. It is not meant to be read. The purpose is to show the color and the size of this type face in the layout. This is dummy copy. It is not meant to be read. The purpose is to show the color and size of this type face in the layout. This is dummy copy. It is not meant to be read. The purpose is to show the color and size This is dummy copy. It is not meant to be read. The purpose is to show the color and the size of this type face in the layout. This is dummy copy. It is not meant to be read. The purpose is to show the color and size of this type face in the layout. This is dummy copy. It is not meant to be read. The purpose is to show the color and size This is dummy copy. It is not meant to be read. The purpose is to show the color and the size of this type face in the layout. This is dummy copy. It is not meant to be read. The purpose is to show the color and size of this type face in the layout. This is dummy copy. It is not meant to be read. The purpose is to show the color and size

Alexandra Guzek

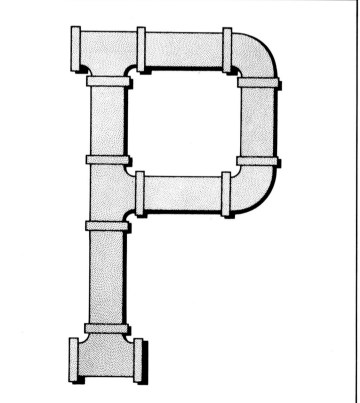

Peter Aguanno

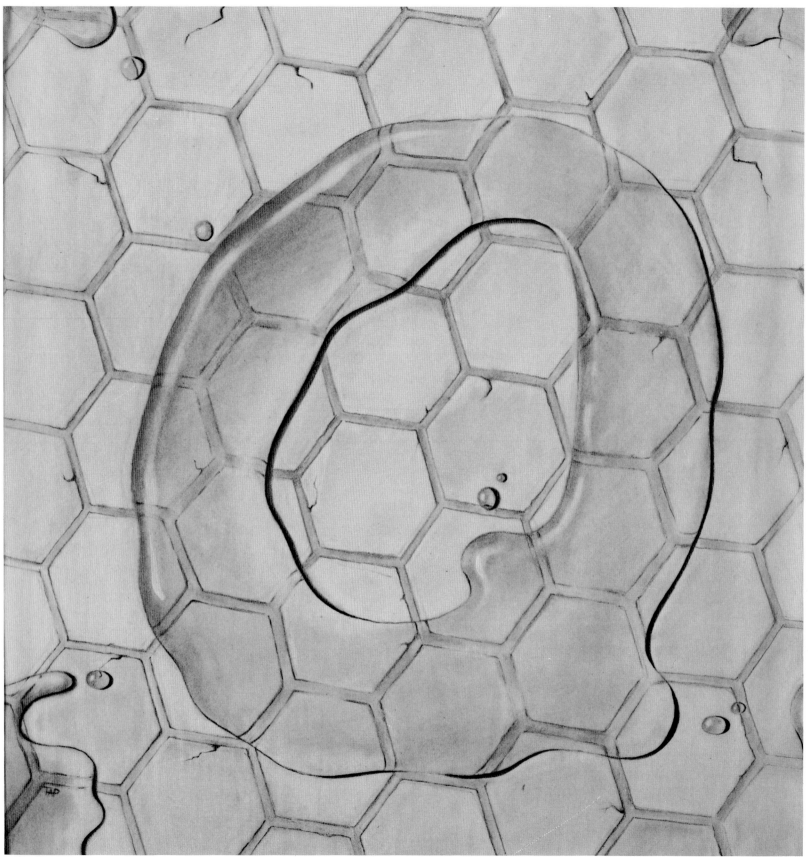

Lorene Tapellini

Roberto Klachky

Benjamin Herskowitz

tttttttttttttttt (bing!)
tttttt....

Tony Ho

Marianne Bosshart

Anusorn Vivathanachai

38

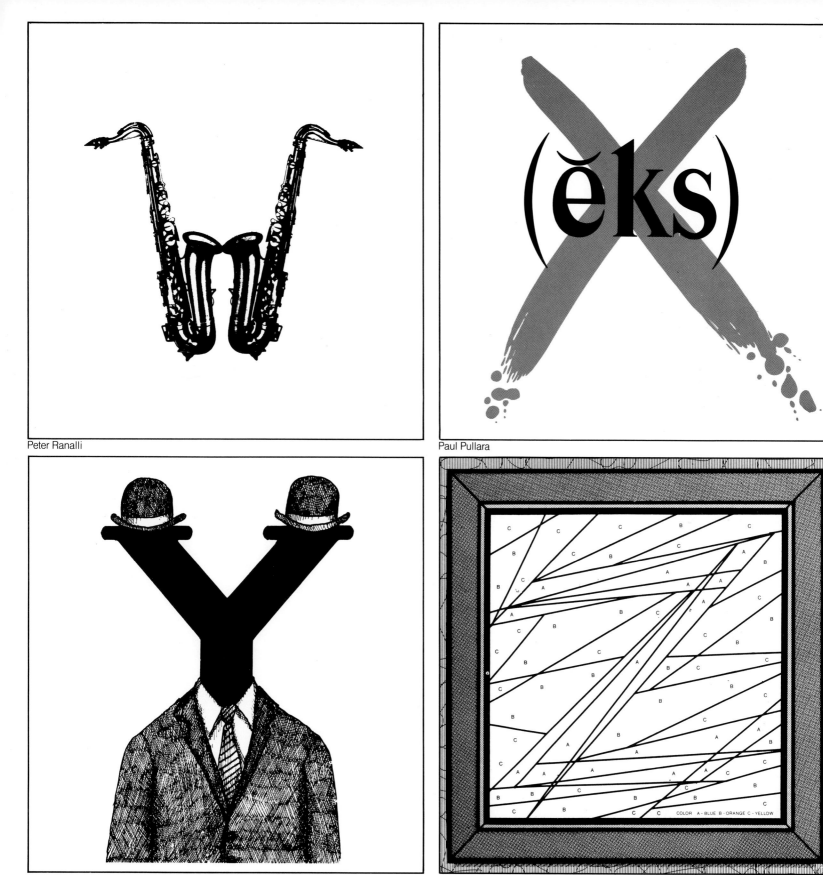

Peter Ranalli

Paul Pullara

Anne Sprague

Rita Dubas

PROBLEM: PUNCTUATION MARK
(Variation of "Alphabet Analogy" Problem)

Although punctuation is an integral part of typography, it is often almost invisible. Choose a single punctuation mark. Extend the possibilities inherent in its form to make it more visible.

SPECIFICATIONS

Size: 6½ by 6½ inches.
Color: Black and white.
Medium: No limitation.
Note: Line or tone solutions are acceptable.

SOLUTION:

Peter Ranalli

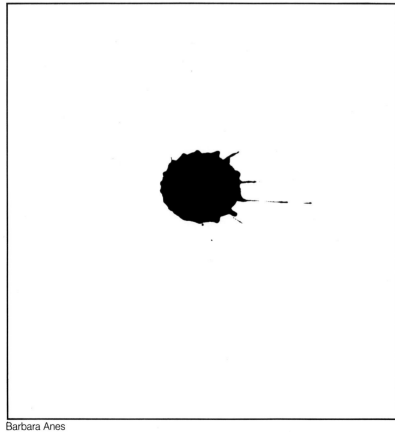

Barbara Anes

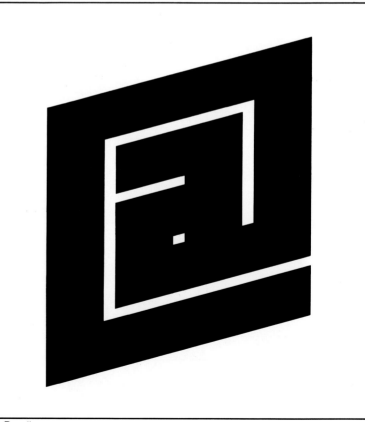

Ernie Rawding

40

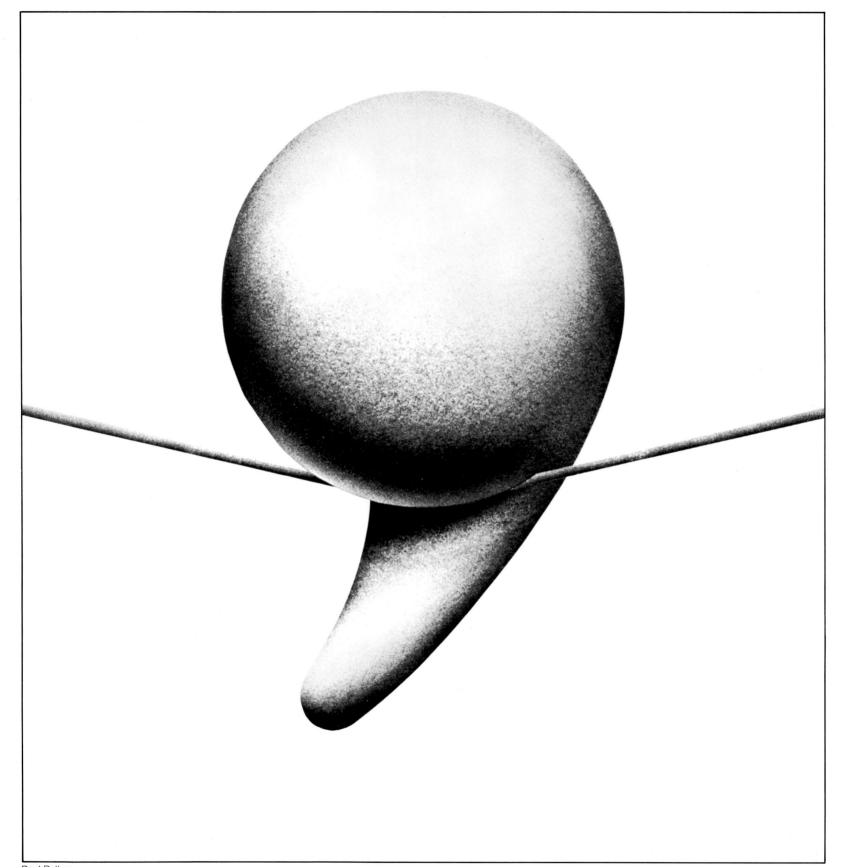

Paul Pullara

PROBLEM: ALPHABET ANALOGY–DESIGNER'S TOOL
(Variation of "Alphabet Analogy" Problem)

Choose any graphic design tool (for example, a pencil, eraser, or ink bottle) and transform it into a letterform. The integrity of both the tool and the type-face must be maintained in creating a successful solution.

SPECIFICATIONS

Size: 6½ by 6½ inches maximum.
Color: Black and white.
Medium: No limitation
Note: Line or tone solutions are acceptable.
Suggestions: The designer's tool itself might suggest a particular letterform.

SOLUTION:

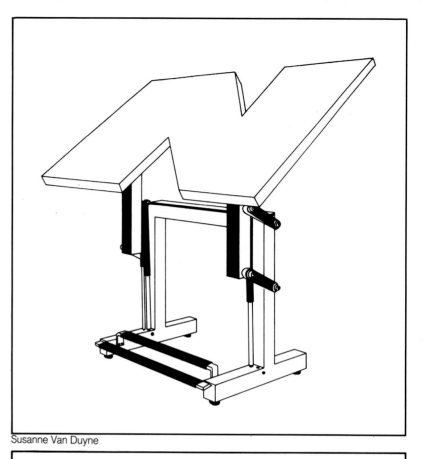

Susanne Van Duyne

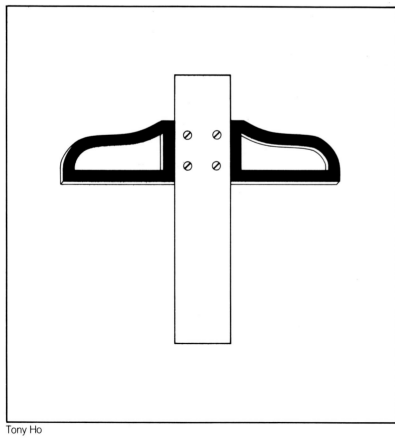

Tony Ho

42

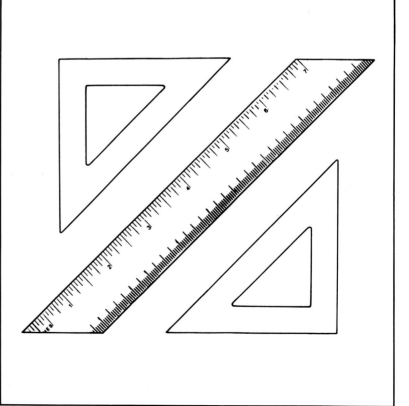

Osnat Zaken

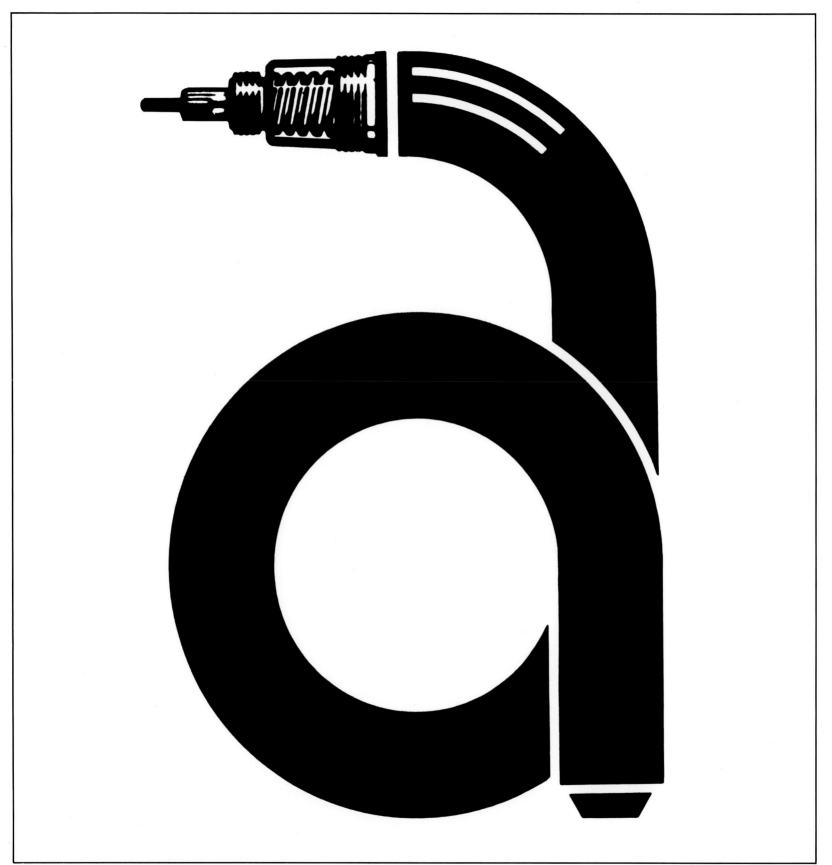

Peter Aguanno

PROBLEM: HEAD AND BODY MONTAGE

Create a life-size portrait using two famous person-alities by juxtaposing the head of one onto the body of the other. As you look at the newly created "per-son," you will respond to both your traditional image of each personality and to the newly formed altered image.

Altering images in this way, combining the ex-pected with the unexpected, has the power to hold attention. This is one of the prerequisites of effective communication. Attracting someone's attention even for seconds is a most desired result in the commu-nication world, where each day thousands of im-ages are vying for consideration.

SPECIFICATIONS

Size: 4 by 6 feet.
Color: Full color.
Medium: Oil paint or acrylic on canvas or Masonite.
Option: Stereotypes can be substituted for the famous personalities.

TITLES:

1. Agnew/Tweedledum
2. Baby/Blue-collar worker
3. Burt Reynolds/Io
4. Napoleon Bonaparte/Marlene Dietrich

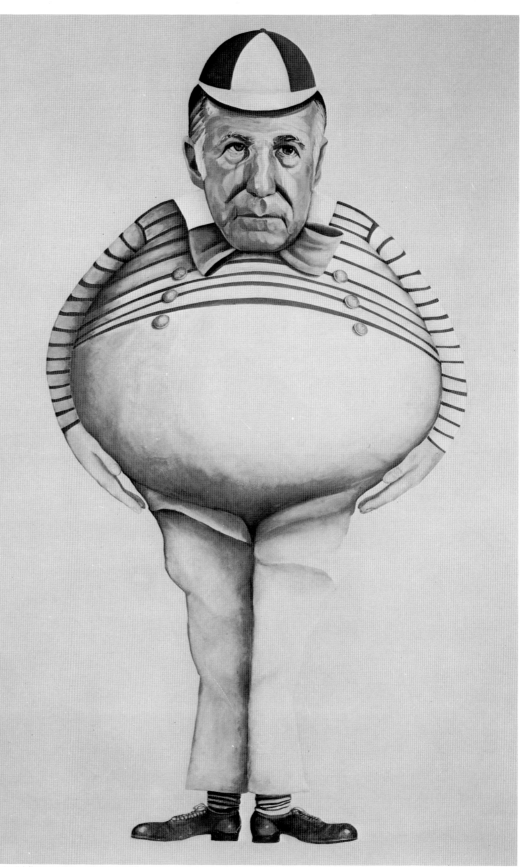

1. Judi Mintzer

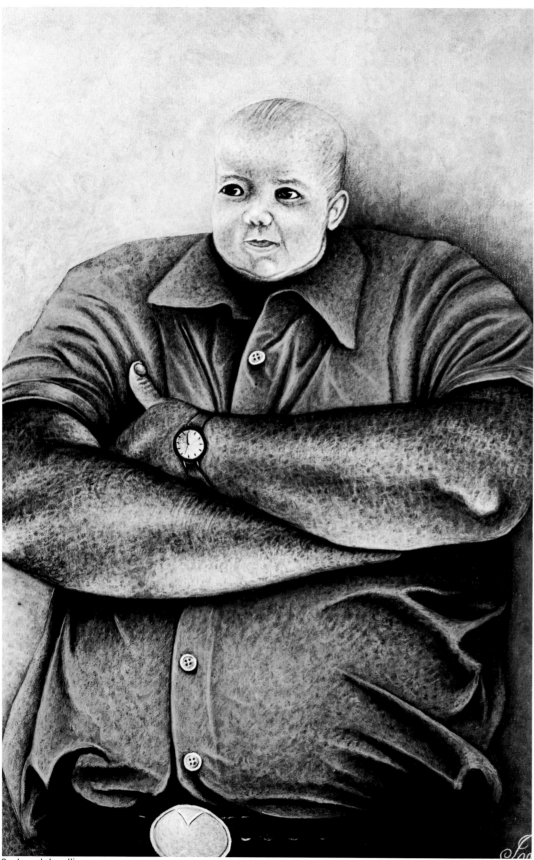

2. Joseph Ianelli

3. Stan Sisson

4. Unknown

45

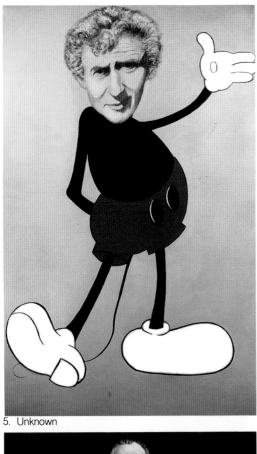

5. Unknown

6. Unknown

7. Salvatore Aprea

8. James Woods

SOLUTION:

5. Norman Mailer/Mickey Mouse
6. Godfather/Pope Paul VI
7. Pope Paul VI/Rolls Royce
8. Groucho Marx/Edouard Manet's *The Fifer*

Identify twenty different characteristics of children in a grade-school class. These should be either emotional or physical characteristics, for example, nervousness or timidness, class pet or class bully. Using the basic elements of a standard notebook page, convey the twenty characteristics you've identified. In redesigning the notebook page, you can alter the space between lines, increase or decrease the thickness of the lines, or change the direction of the lines. The only limitation is that you do not completely destroy the basic identity of the notebook page. Draw your solutions in the areas indicated. Using the large rectangle at the top of the assignment sheet, convey the personality of the teacher.

You may choose to redesign a sheet of loose-leaf paper instead of a sheet of notebook paper. If you choose loose-leaf paper, the holes should be included as a design element.

SPECIFICATIONS

Size: As indicated on assignment sheet.
Color: Red and blue.
Medium: Ink or colored pencils.
Copy: Although titles are not necessary, indicate the personality of each solution on the reverse side of the assignment.

The Notebook Problem: The standard page in a grade school notebook is a sheet of white paper, printed with blue lines and a red double lined margin (see sample). Utilizing the basic elements of the notebook page create a personality for 20 different children in a grade school class. The personality that you create should reflect emotional or physical characteristics. For example: nervousness, timidness, class pet, class bully, etc. In redesigning the notebook page, you can alter the space between lines, increase or decrease the thickness of the lines, change the direction of the lines, etc. The only limitation is that you do not completely destroy the basic identity of the notebook page. Draw your solutions, in the 20 rectangles below. Using the large rectangle at the top of the page, create a personality for the teacher of the class. Note: you must follow the rules outlined above. Option: You may choose to redesign a sheet of loose leaf paper instead of a sheet of notebook paper. If you choose loose leaf paper the holes should be included in your design.

Sample

School of Visual Arts

Produced by the Visual Arts Press. This is an experimental project created by the Media Arts Department of the School of Visual Arts, 209 East 23rd Street, New York City 10010.

SOLUTION:

TITLES:

Unbalanced
Teacher

Row 1

Shy	Average	Loud-mouth	Smartest	Four-eyes

Row 2

Fat	Empty-headed	Day-dreamer	Love Bird	Love Bird

Row 3

Introverted	Frustrated	Slob	Lazy	Nervous

Row 4

Lethargic	Tall	Non-conformist	Clown	Bully

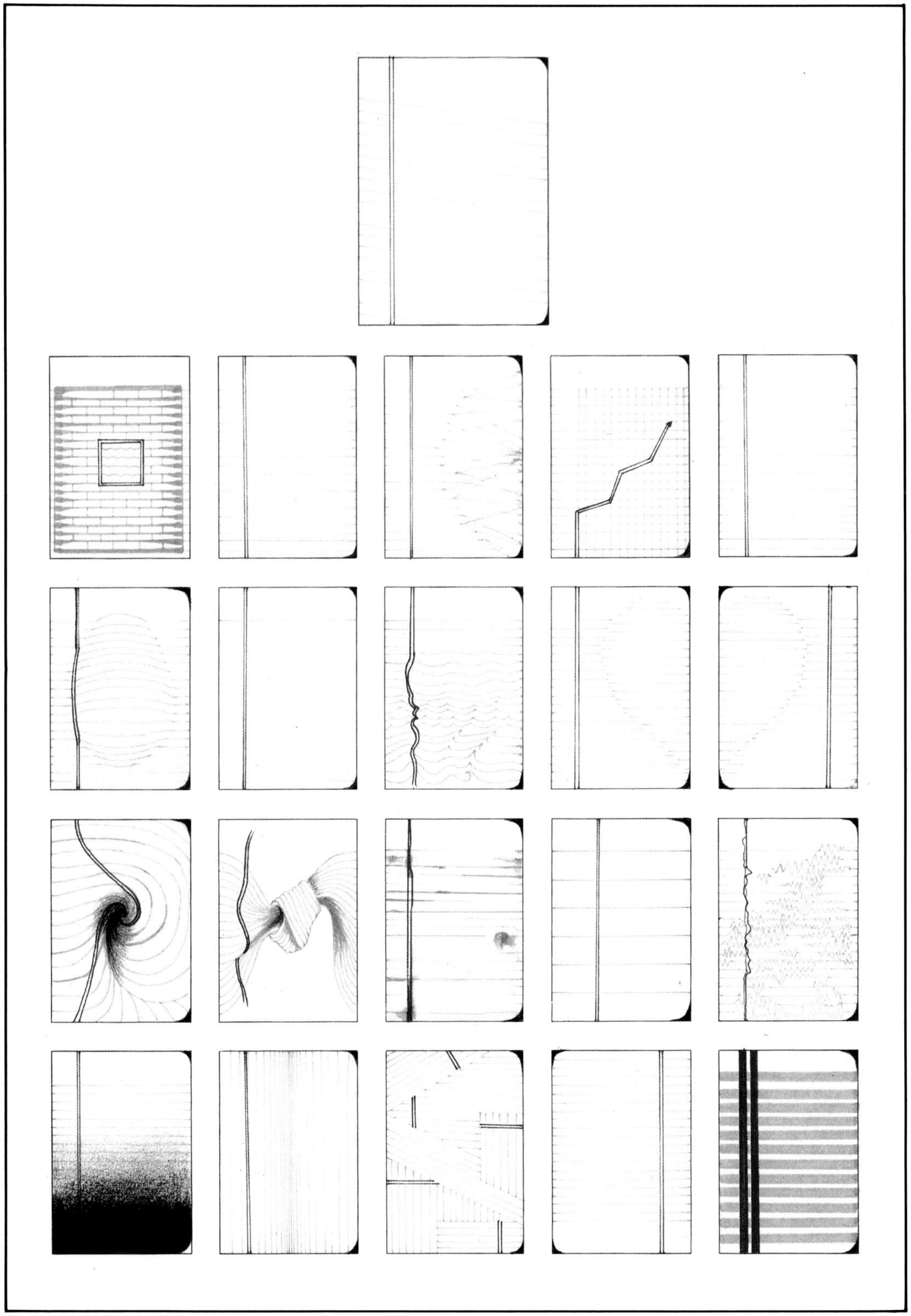

Carlos Nicholls

49

SOLUTION:

TITLES:

Substitute
Teacher

Row 1

Confused Blind Aggressive Nearsighted Tardy

Row 2

Timid Oriental Computer Egocentric Rigid
       Student   Wiz

Row 3

Bashful Tease Flirt Copy- Precise
                       cat

Row 4

Doodler Absent- Expelled Girl in Love Boy in Love
         minded   Delinquent

Xavier Wasowski

50

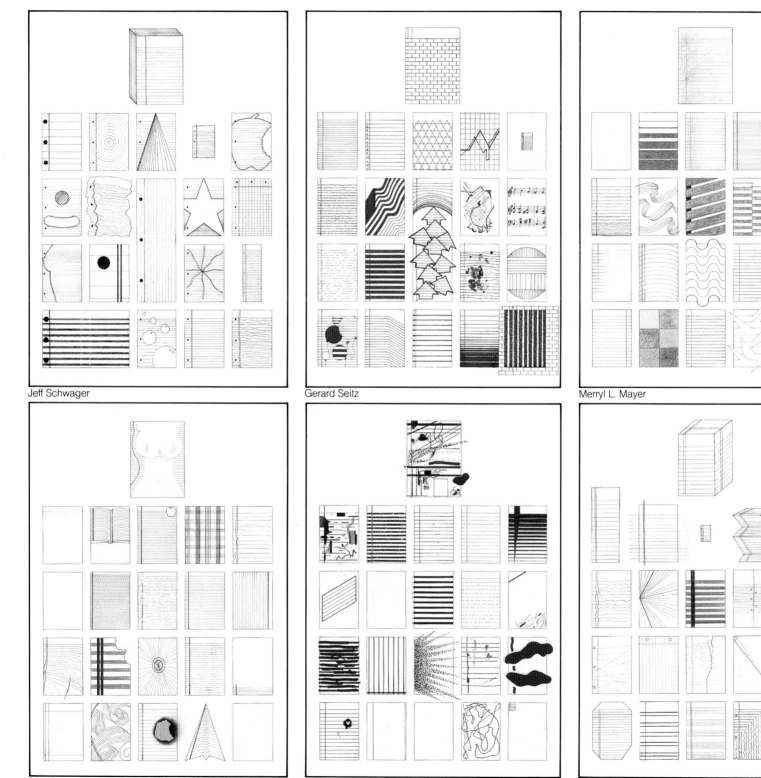

Jeff Schwager

Gerard Seitz

Merryl L. Mayer

Jeff Durham

Steve Ouditt

Jean Farrel Miles

SOLUTION:

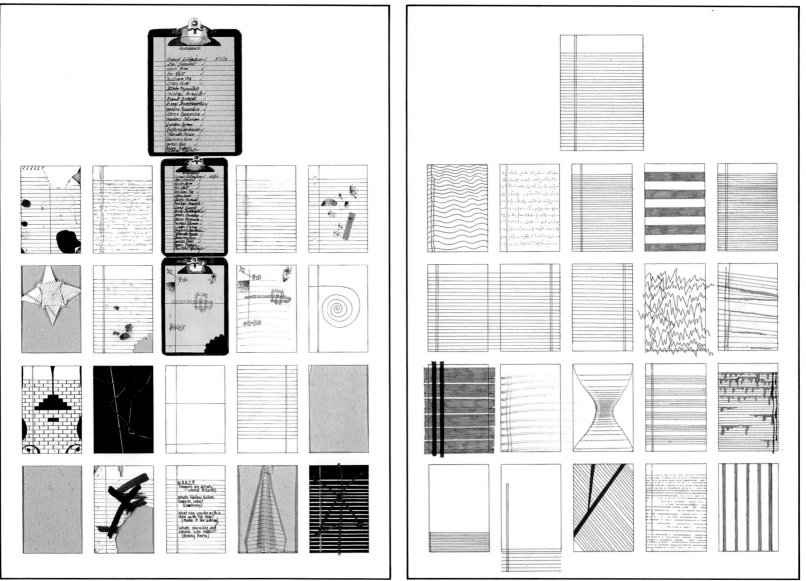

Joyce Novotny

Jace Dawson

52

SINGLE SOLUTIONS:

TITLES:
1. Lags Behind
2. Class Patsy
3. Video Addict
4. Studious
5. Gum Chewer
6. Child Wearing Baseball Cap

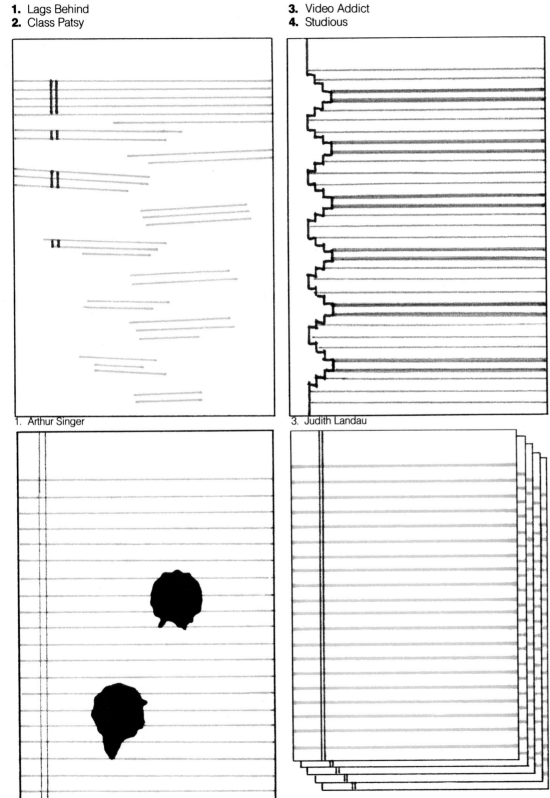

1. Arthur Singer

3. Judith Landau

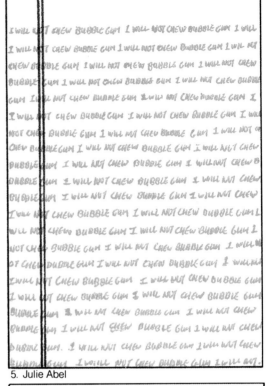

5. Julie Abel

2. Jim McKeon

4. Bryan Thatcher

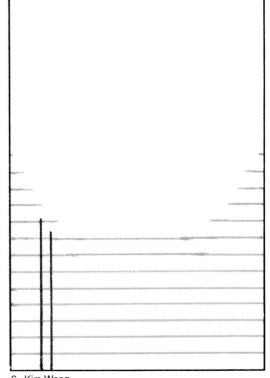

6. Kim Wong

SINGLE SOLUTIONS:

TITLES:

1. Musician
2. Troublemaker
3. Daydreamer
4. Drug User

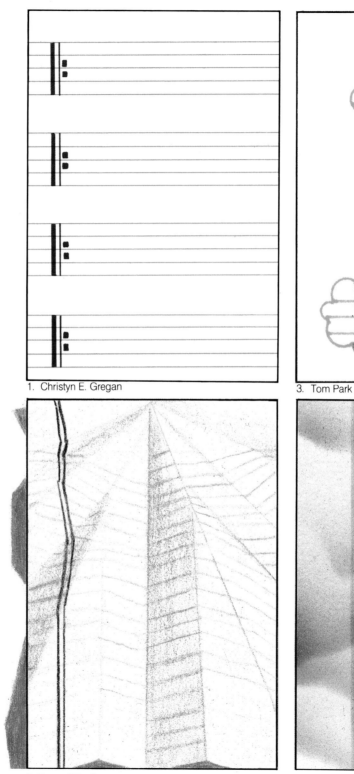

1. Christyn E. Gregan

3. Tom Park

2. Duane Ulisnik

4. Sandra Harris

SOLUTION:

SINGLE SOLUTIONS:

5. Self-centered
6. Computer Brain

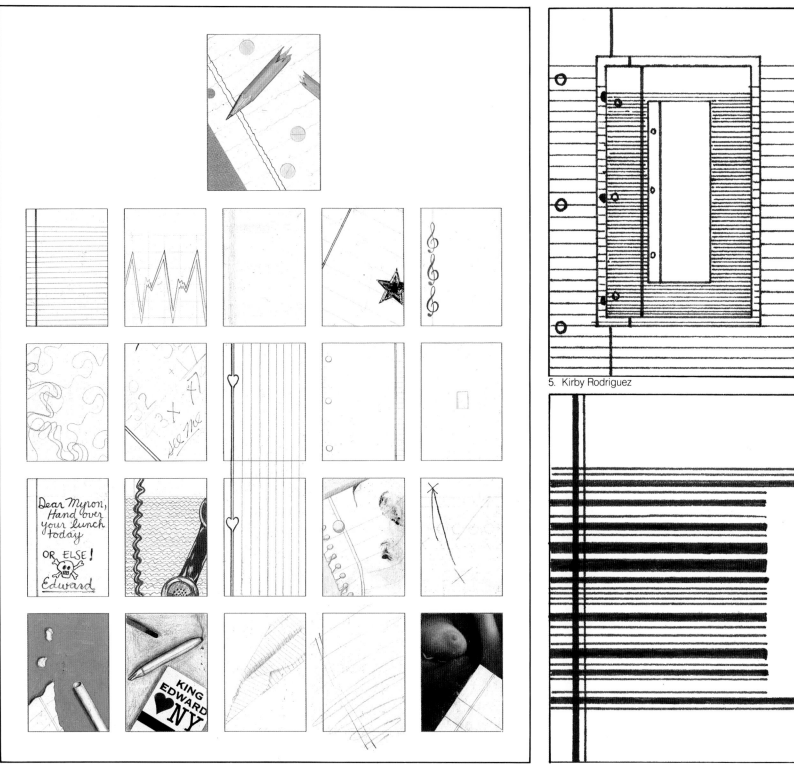

John William Costa

5. Kirby Rodriguez

6. Kirby Rodriguez

55

SINGLE SOLUTIONS:

TITLES:

1. Richard Wilde (Teacher)
2. Coffee Fiend (Teacher)
3. Dictator (Teacher)
4. Nervous Breakdown (Teacher)

1. David S. Rocchio

3. Paul H. Devejian

2. Lisa M. Rosel

4. Toby Fox

5. Troublemaker
6. Crybaby

7. Boisterous
8. Farsighted

9. Class Slut
10. Color-blind

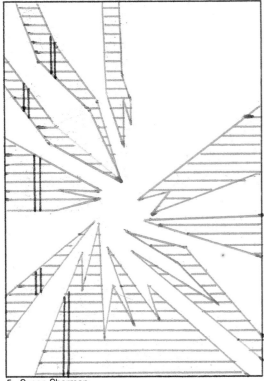

5. Susan Sherman

7. John Dardani

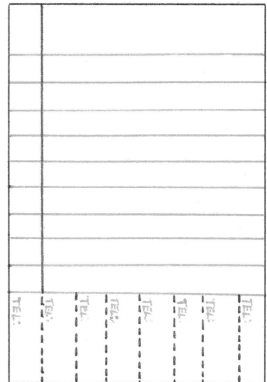

9. Kimberly Fulcher

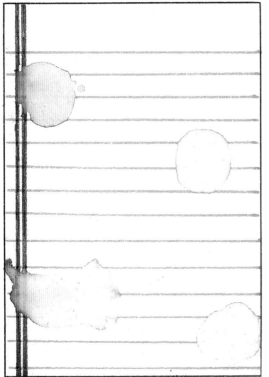

6. Annika Larsson

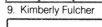

8. Joanne Gonzalez

10. Tom Godici

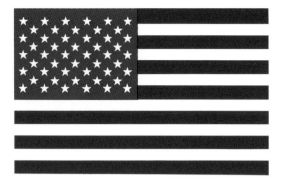

Redesign the American flag to make a personal statement about a political or social issue in the United States. In order to maintain a connection between the traditional flag and your new design, you must use stars and stripes and the colors red, white, and blue. These limitations provide experience in using purely graphic elements to resolve a design problem.

SPECIFICATIONS

Size: 4 by 6 inches.
Color: Red and blue, plus additional colors as necessary.
Medium: No limitation.
Ground: White, any material.

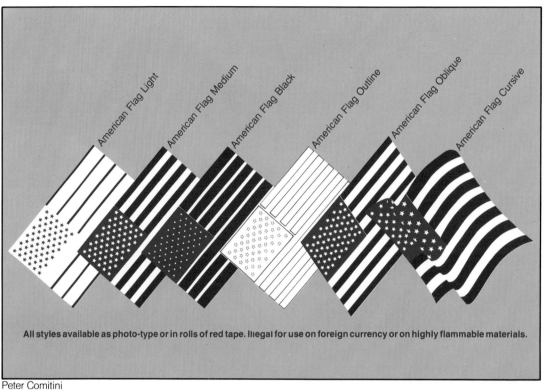

Peter Comitini

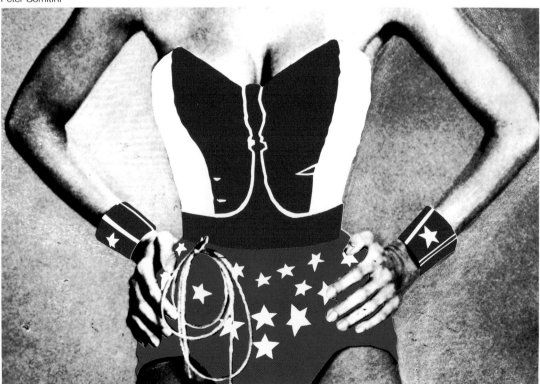

Eileen Rafferty

Steven Kaufman

Peter Comitini

Jackie Vaccaro

SOLUTION:

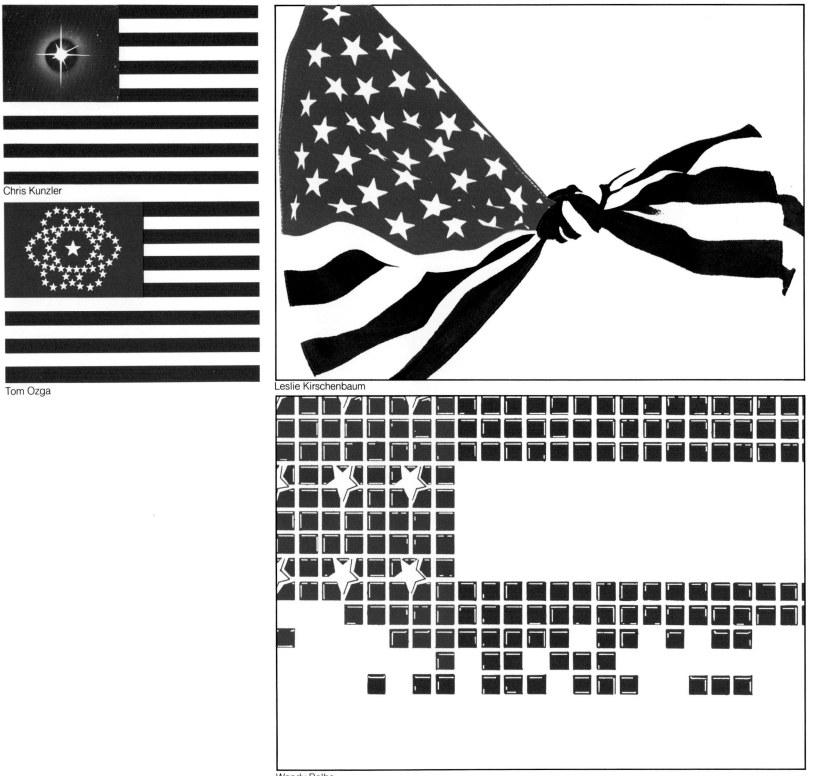

Chris Kunzler

Tom Ozga

Leslie Kirschenbaum

Wendy Balbo

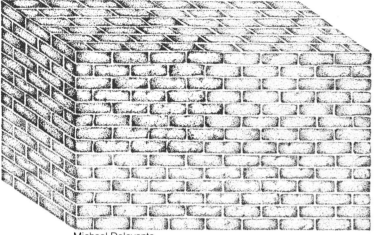
Michael Delevante

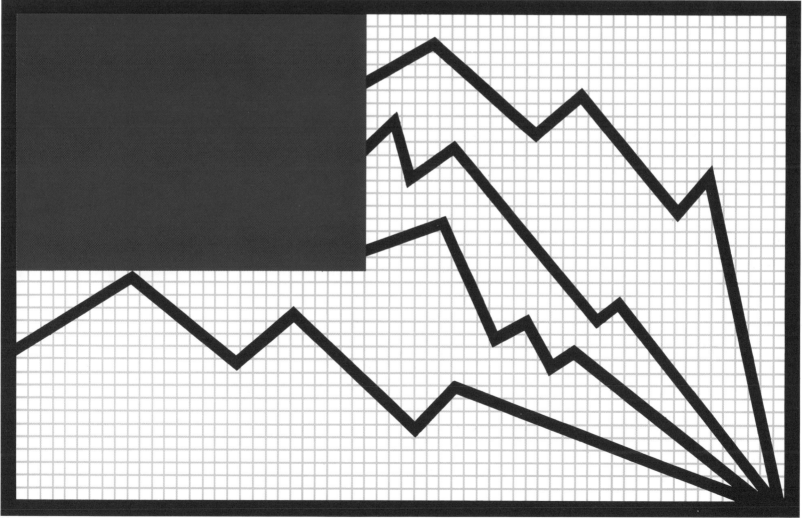
Margaret Bruen

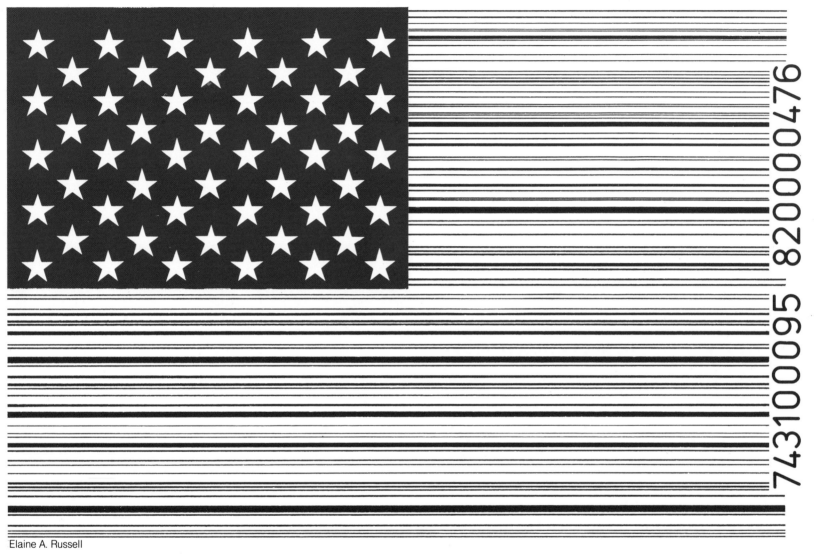

Elaine A. Russell

Tom Ozga

SOLUTION:

Joseph DePinho

Eileen Rafferty

Pat Watkins

Robyn Kossoff

Jane Tarallo

PROBLEM: THE POSTAGE STAMP SERIES

When you express a personal issue honestly, you usually touch an audience much larger than yourself. You have to dare to work in this way. Delving into yourself for a solution results in more than an effective design—you will learn about yourself as well as about visual communication. This represents a true learning situation.

The following six postage stamp problems are extensions of this idea. All had the same specifications, as listed below.

SPECIFICATIONS

Size: 4 by 4 inches.
Color: Full color.
Medium: No limitation.
Requirement: Design a simulated perforation.
Option: Copy, name of country, and monetary denominations may be used.

PROBLEM: NONTRADITIONAL STAMP

Using the traditional postage stamp format, create a U.S. stamp that incorporates a nontraditional yet personal theme.

SOLUTION:

SAMPLE PROBLEM:

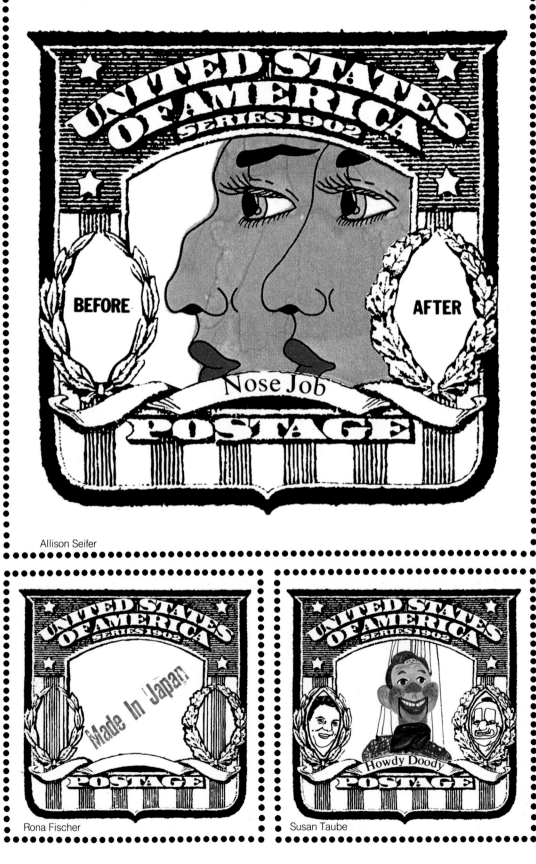

Allison Seifer

Rona Fischer

Susan Taube

PROBLEM: FOOD STAMP

The United States is the fattest nation in the world—it has the largest population of overweight people. Design a stamp that illustrates this dubious fact.

SOLUTION:

Tetsuya Matsuura

Bill Kobasz

Fran Newman

Shelly Clifford

Chris Bobbin

Scott Fishoff

PROBLEM: POLITICAL STAMP

PROBLEM: ALL-AMERICAN STAMP

Choose a significant political issue, past or present. Research the issue thoroughly. Then assimilate the facts and express your view of the issue symbolically, in the form of a postage stamp.

Using the elements of the American flag, create a stamp that makes a personal statement about the United States.

SOLUTION: ⟩

SOLUTION:

Paula Greif

Hiroaki Ohta

Kevin Unick

Howard Liebman

Naomi Sacher

Linda Davis

Robin Battino

Beverly Haw

Takao Matsumoto

Laura O'Brien

David Montiel

Alida Beck

PROBLEM: PERSONAL STAMP

Depict an issue that is uniquely personal, using the
form of a postage stamp. Topics may range from the
commonplace to the abstract.

SOLUTION:

Sue Cucinotta

Jo Sondheim

Kimberley Sandhagen

Patrick McDonnell

Beat Keller

Tina Strasberg

PROBLEM: BICENTENNIAL STAMP

Using a stamp as a way of marking time, create an image that represents the 200th birthday of the United States of America. This image should represent your personal interpretation of this historic event.

SOLUTION:

UNITED STATES OF AMERICA

1776 • BICENTENNIAL • 1976

Jacqui Bonavito

USA • 1976

Gillian Smith

Julie Wowk

PROBLEM: HEART PLUS THE LETTER *H*

SOLUTION:

Relating two graphic elements in a given space is a fundamental design concept that can form the basis for solving all types of graphic design problems. Create a design that incorporates the symbol of a heart and the letter *H*. The heart and the letter *H* should be used to express a personal vision. At the same time you are relating the heart to the *H*, consider a third element, the background (essentially defined by the outer edge of the page), which is an intrinsic part of any design solution.

To resolve this problem, draw a minimum of thirty thumbnail sketches. Choose the best three thumbnails and work them up into full-size comprehensive drawings. Refine the best comp to simulate a printed piece.

NOTE: Drawings A, B, and C are examples of the prerequisite sketches.

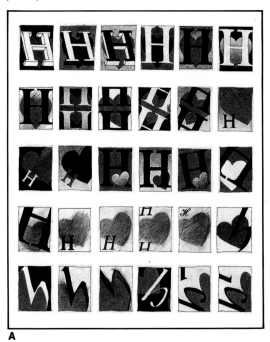

A

SPECIFICATIONS

Size: 4 by 6 inches.
Color: Red and black.
Ground: White, any material.
Medium: Pen and ink, dyes, colored pencils, colored films, colored paper, or airbrush.

Merryl L. Mayer

B

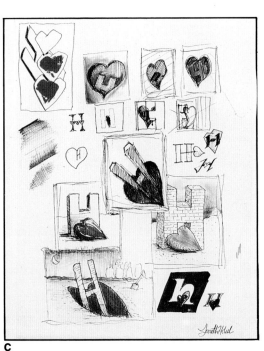

C

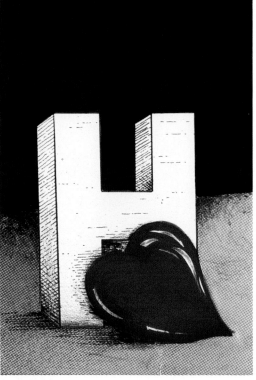

Jareth Holub

74

Isabella Fasciano

Scott Frommer

Jace Dawson

Vivian Pinida

Tom Godici

Timothy O'Keefe

PROBLEM: CROSSWORD PUZZLE MAGAZINE COVER

SOLUTION:

This assignment offers an opportunity to explore the use of symmetry as a design element. Because symmetry brings a sense of expected order to a design, it seems too obvious, sometimes too boring, a solution, and we tend to shy away from its use. Yet, precisely because it creates a sense of expected order, symmetry can be an effective design solution. Human beings are physically symmetrical, and we have an intrinsic ability to recognize and relate to the visual symmetry that surrounds us. It mirrors our own image. Consider using symmetry as a vehicle to express your ideas.

If you examine a crossword puzzle blank, you will see that one-half of the grid mirrors the other; it is symmetrical. In three colors plus black, use the pattern of a crossword puzzle to design a cover for a crossword puzzle magazine. By experimenting with percentages and the overlapping of colors, you can gain an appreciation of the wide range of color possibilities that can be used to create a more effective solution. This type of design problem allows you to explore the technical side of graphic design.

SPECIFICATIONS

Size: Image size: 5 by 5 inches.
Page size: 6 by 9 inches. (Image is to be centered horizontally and placed ½ inch from bottom of page.)
Color: Four colors, one of which must be black.
Medium: Pen and ink, dyes, colored pencils, colored films, colored paper, or airbrush.
Note: In the advanced version of this assignment, a masthead for the magazine would be designed.

Sandra Bella

Adam Garfinkel

Christian C. Fencht

Greg Pedersen

PROBLEM: CROSSWORD PUZZLE MAGAZINE COVER (Variation of original problem)

Follow the instructions for the preceding problem but incorporate a pencil as a design element.

SOLUTION:

Scott Wadler

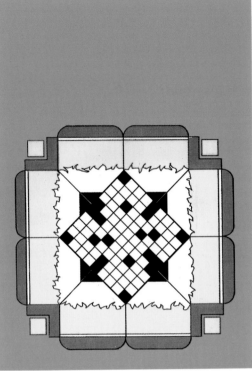

Christine Lee

Sik Wang Yu

PROBLEM: GRAFFITI

Although graffiti is generally condemned as a defacement of public property, some consider it a viable artform. Choose two famous personalities and apply graffiti to the top and middle subway cars to represent their personalities. Apply graffiti to the bottom car to express your own personality.

SPECIFICATIONS

Size: As indicated on the assignment sheet.
Color: Full color or black and white.
Medium: Any medium, including spray paint.
Copy: Although not required, copy may be used as a design element. To avoid any confusion as to the identities of your chosen personalities, indicate their names on the reverse side of the assignment sheet.
Note: Remember that you are working on the surface of a train and that the train's structure can be incorporated into your design.

TITLES:

1. Vincent van Gogh
2. Piet Mondrian
3. Self-portrait
4. Self-portrait

SAMPLE PROBLEM:

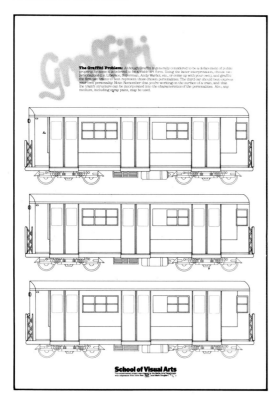

SINGLE SOLUTIONS:

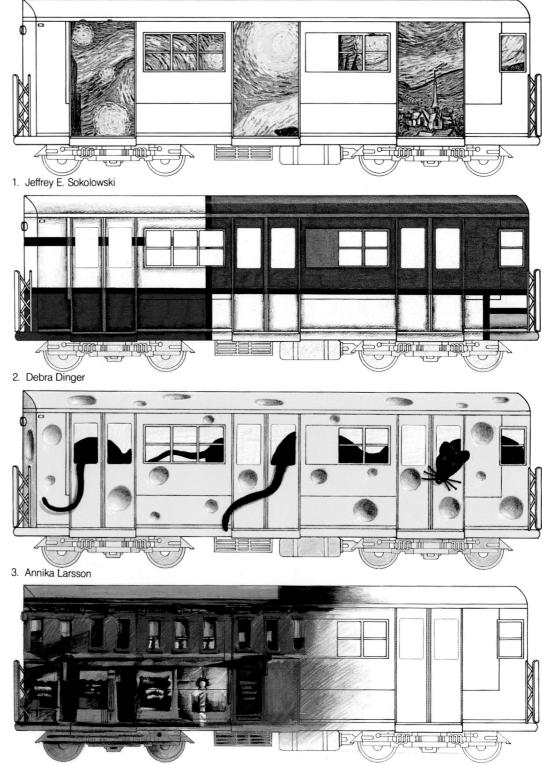

1. Jeffrey E. Sokolowski

2. Debra Dinger

3. Annika Larsson

4. Gary Pratico

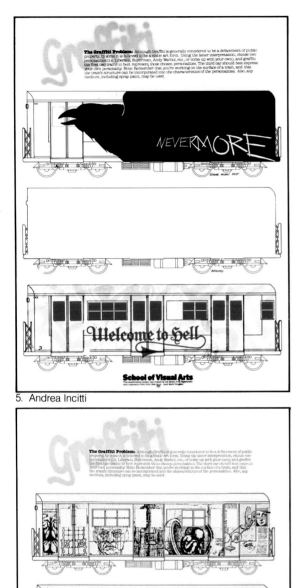

5. Andrea Incitti

6. Scott Ballew

5. a. Edgar Allen Poe
   b. The Invisible Man
   c. Self-portrait
6. a. Leonardo da Vinci
   b. The Beatles
   c. Self-portrait
7. Caveman
8. Albert Einstein
9. Monty Hall

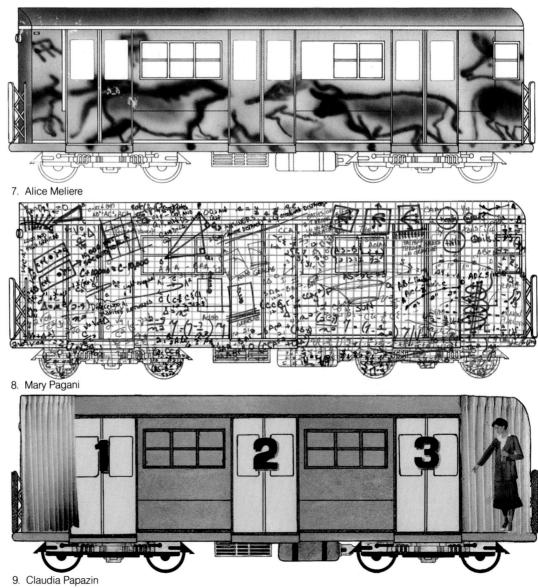

7. Alice Meliere

8. Mary Pagani

9. Claudia Papazin

SINGLE SOLUTIONS:

10. a. Henri Matisse
   b. Andy Warhol
   c. Self-portrait
11. John D. Rockefeller
12. Self-portrait
13. Self-portrait
14. Self-portrait

11. Hanan Fissay

12. Kam Mak

10. Merryl L. Mayer

14. Leroy Mack

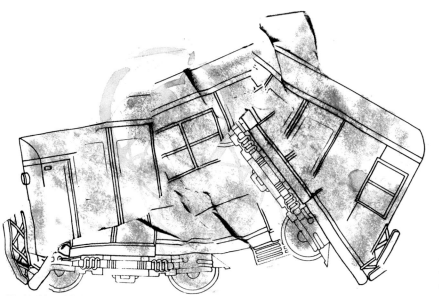

15. Kathleen McMillan

15. Self-portrait
16. Rabbi Jacob Rabbinowitz
17. Christo

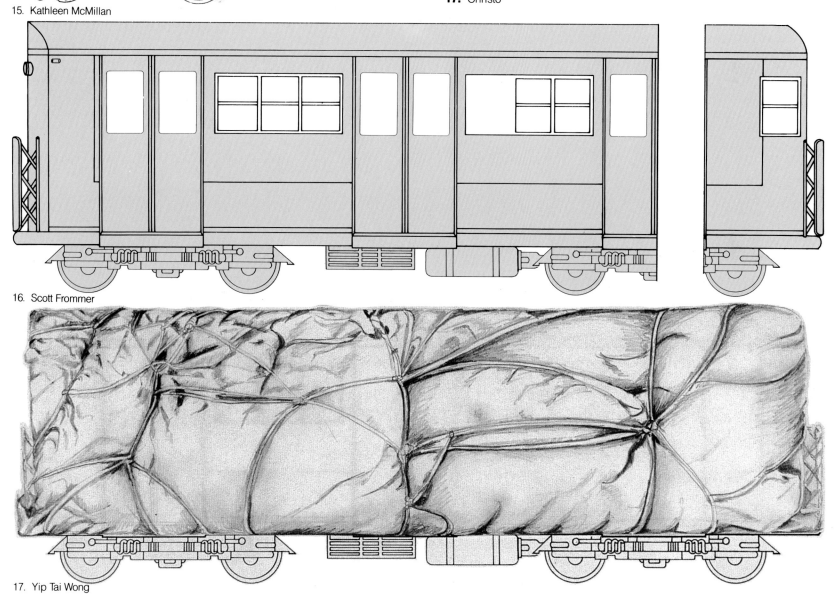

16. Scott Frommer

17. Yip Tai Wong

SINGLE SOLUTIONS:

18. Fred Astaire
19. Elevator Operator

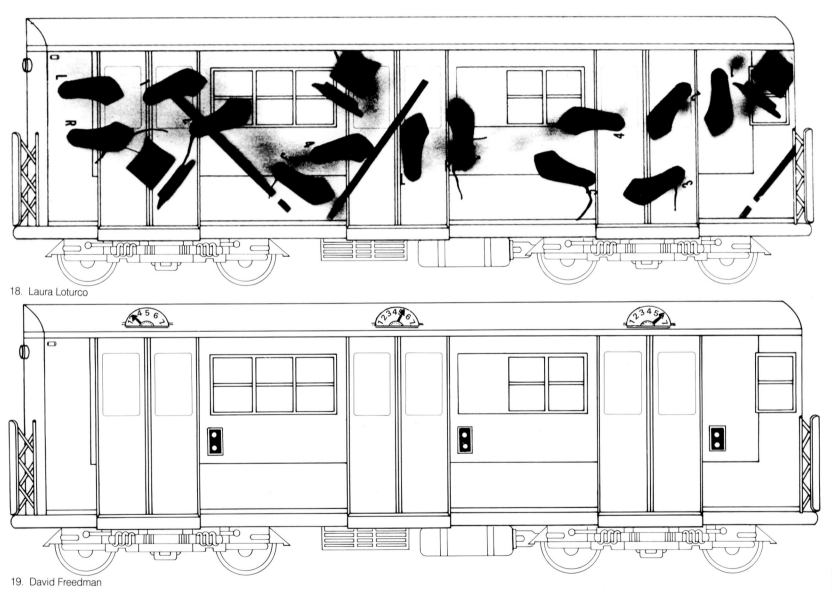

18. Laura Loturco

19. David Freedman

20. **20.** The Old Woman Who Lived in a Shoe
21. Bernhard Goetz
22. King Tut

20. Judy Virsinger

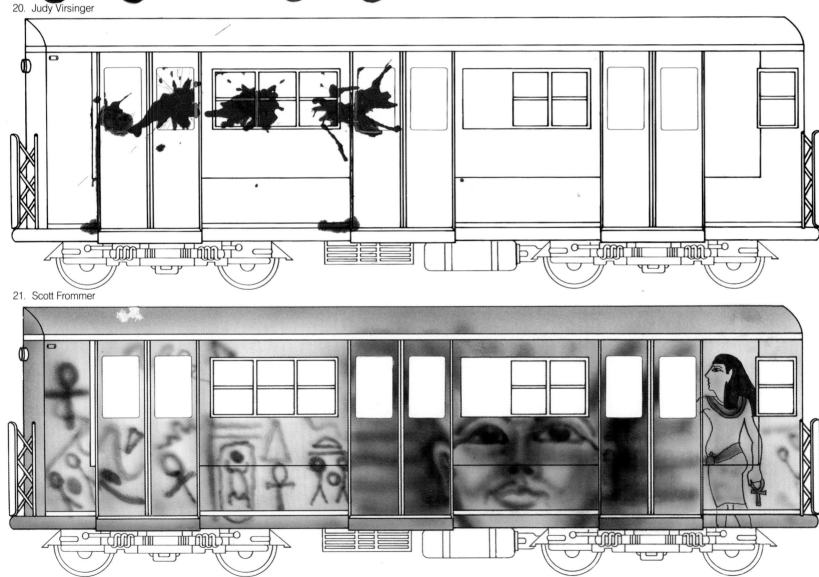

21. Scott Frommer

22. Alice Meliere

SINGLE SOLUTIONS:

23. Robert Motherwell   **25.** Richard Haas
24. Keith Haring   **26.** René Magritte
    27. Jackson Pollock

23. Gabrielle Carter

24. Unknown

84

25. Cathy D'Itallan

26. Mary Dolan

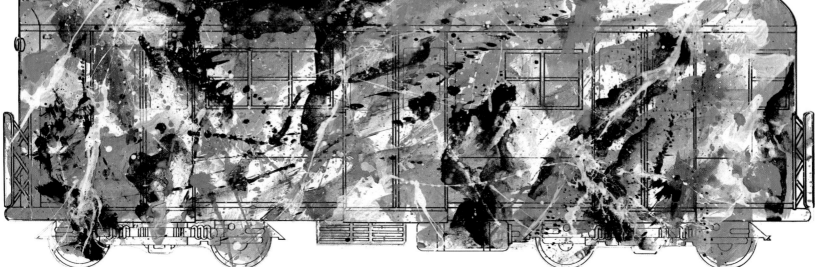

27. Gary Pratico

Invent a piece of correspondence from one party (person, institution, or object) to another, using visual, not verbal, language. The message, which can be of any nature, should convey the relationship between the two parties. The only stipulation is that your message be visual.

This assignment actually presents two challenges: first you must define the problem to be solved by inventing the message; then you must solve it within the confines of a visual letter.

SPECIFICATIONS

Size: As indicated on assignment sheet.
Color: Full color or black and white.
Medium: No limitation.
Copy: Indicate the names of both parties in the appropriate places.

SAMPLE PROBLEM:

Letter Problem Invent a correspondence between two people or an individual and an institution, using visual not verbal language. For example, visualize an appropriate message between Metropolitan Life Insurance and Evel Knievel, Roy Rogers and Trigger, or President Carter and the Peanut Growers Association, etc. The message can be critical, humorous, or satirical. The only stipulation is that your message must be visual instead of verbal.

Dear

"

Sincerely yours,

School of Visual Arts
Produced by the Visual Arts Press. This is an experimental project created by the Media Arts Department of the School of Visual Arts, 209 East 23rd Street, New York City 10010

Jean Farrel Miles

Dear

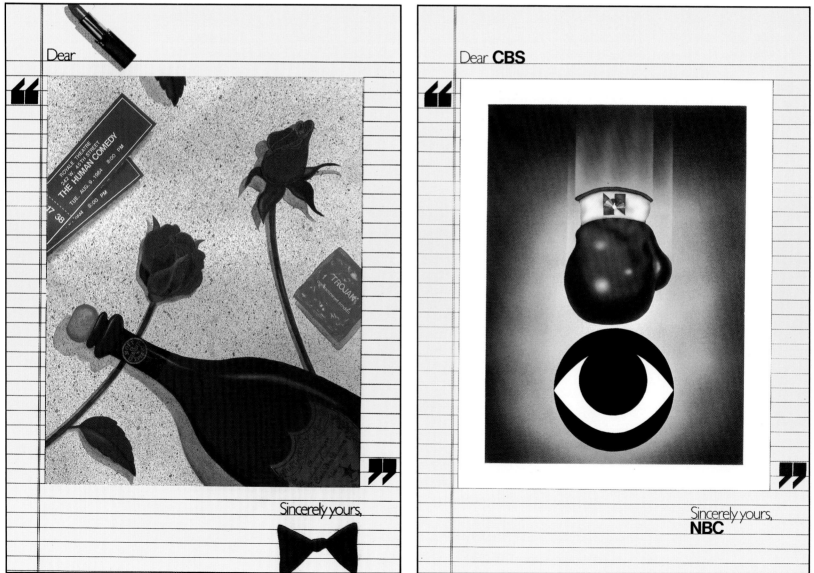

" "

Sincerely yours,

John William Costa

Dear **CBS**

" "

Sincerely yours,
NBC

Greg Pedersen

SOLUTION:

NOTE: In the Visual Letter, problem, topical solutions were encouraged. The solution below is about William Schroeder, who was an artificial-heart recipient.

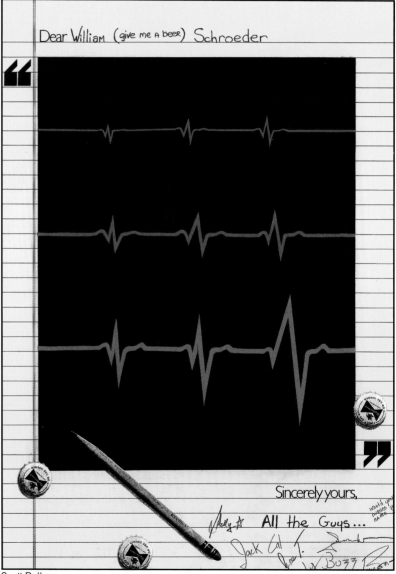

Bob Thornberry

Scott Ballew

88

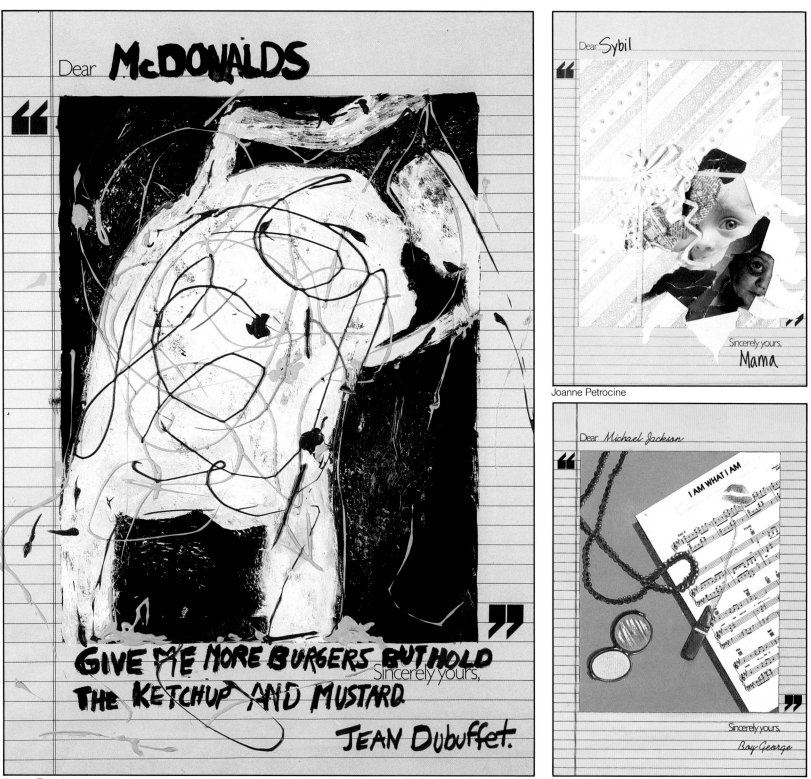

Dear **McDONALDS**

"

"

GIVE ME MORE BURGERS BUT HOLD
THE KETCHUP AND MUSTARD

Sincerely yours,

JEAN Dubuffet.

Joanne Trangle

Dear Sybil

"

Sincerely yours,
Mama

Joanne Petrocine

Dear *Michael Jackson*

"

I AM WHAT I AM

"

Sincerely yours,
Boy George

Katheen Lewandowski

SOLUTION:

NOTE: This letter is from a student to a teacher (who in this case is the originator of the Visual Letter problem). The solution represents wishful thinking.

Kathy Romagnoli

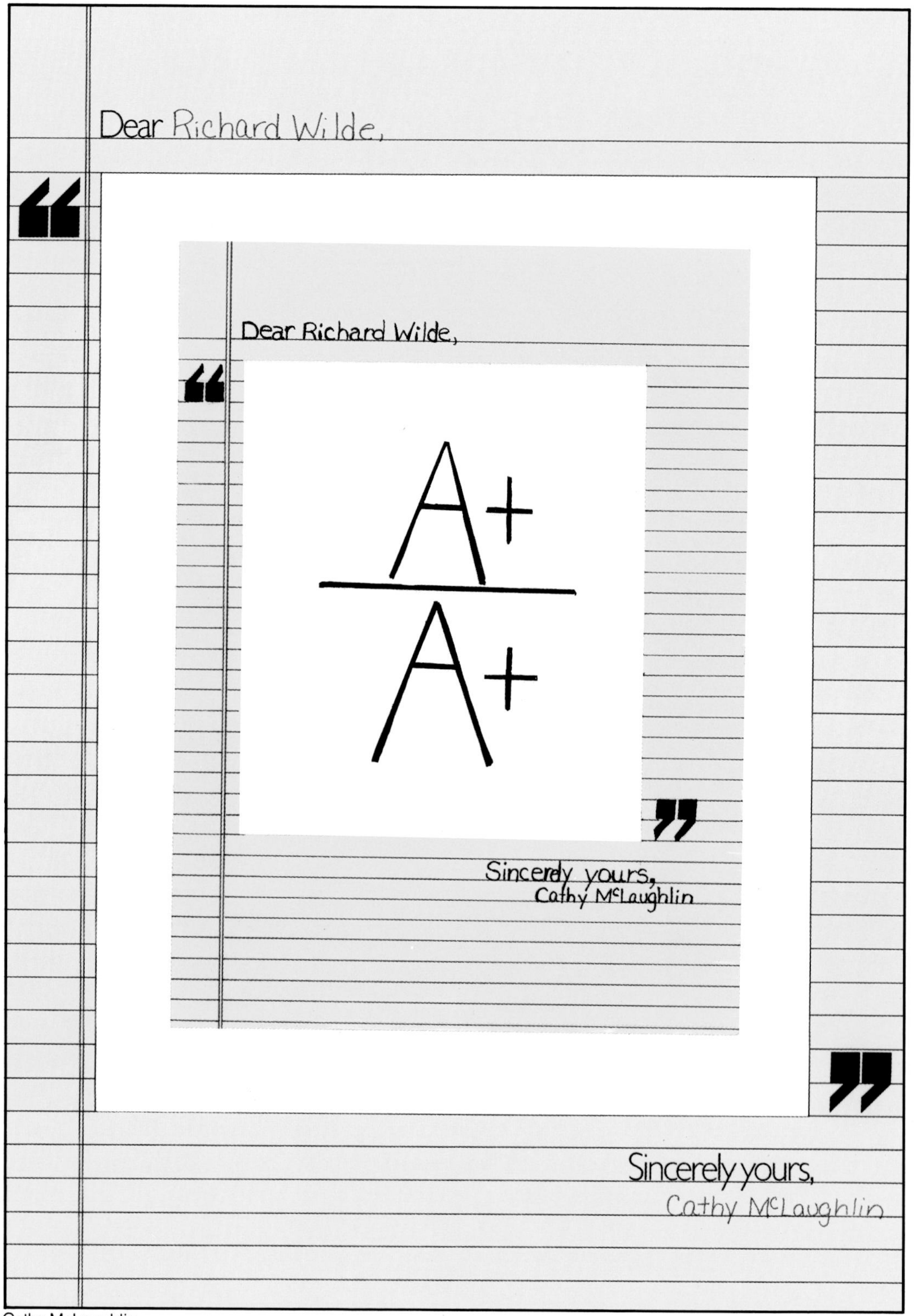

Cathy McLaughlin

90

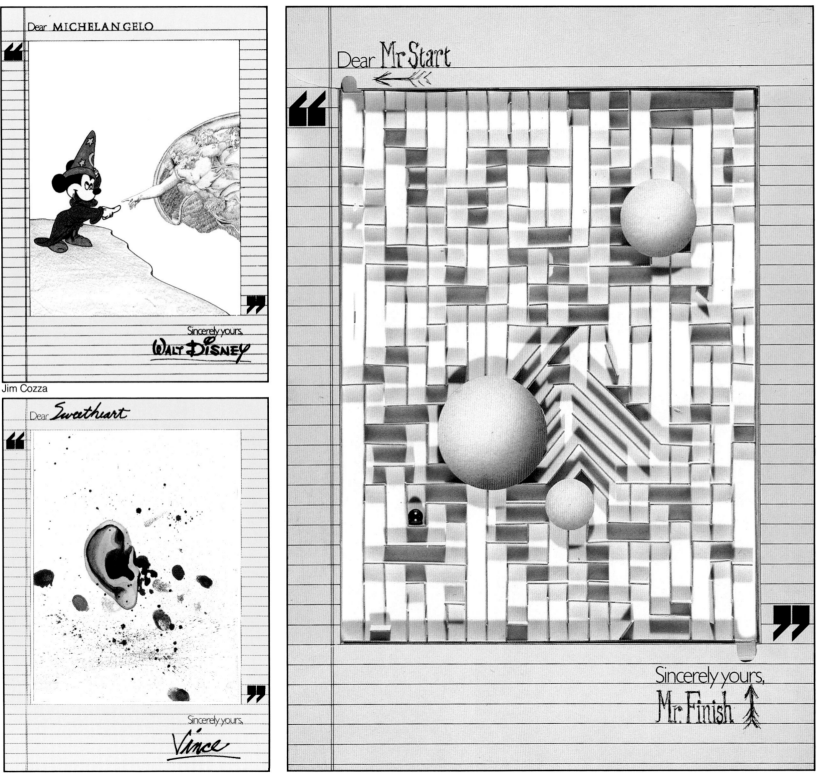

Jim Cozza

Jim Siegel

Ron Leighton

PROBLEM: MOUTH MASK

SOLUTION:

Masks have been part of the ritual and ceremony of many cultures and have religious and esoteric origins. Contemporary masks are mostly devoid of meaning and tradition. They attempt to either frighten or amuse but frequently do not succeed. The assignment is to upgrade the humorous mask, using the mouth as a design element. The mask must be designed on a two-dimensional surface and must be wearable.

SPECIFICATIONS

Size: No restrictions; concept to dictate size and shape.
Color: Full color.
Medium: No limitation.
Requirement: Indicate all perforations, folds, and cutouts.

Pucker Mouth

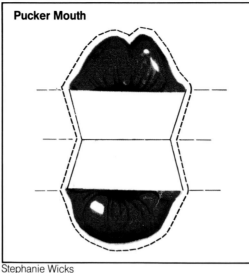

Stephanie Wicks

All-American Mouth

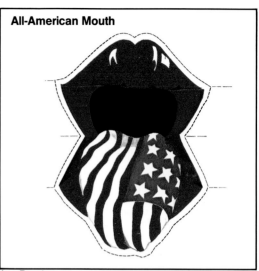

Ann Renzi

Button-Your-Lip Mouth

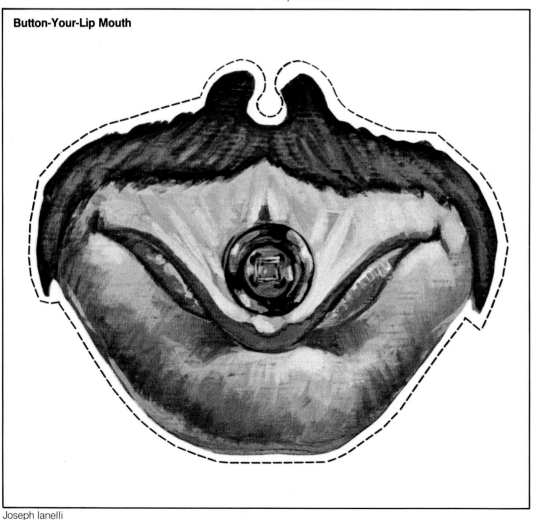

Joseph Ianelli

Shhhh Mouth

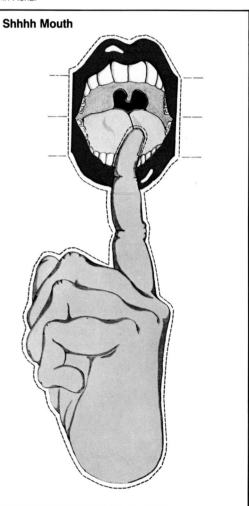

Lana Giganti

92

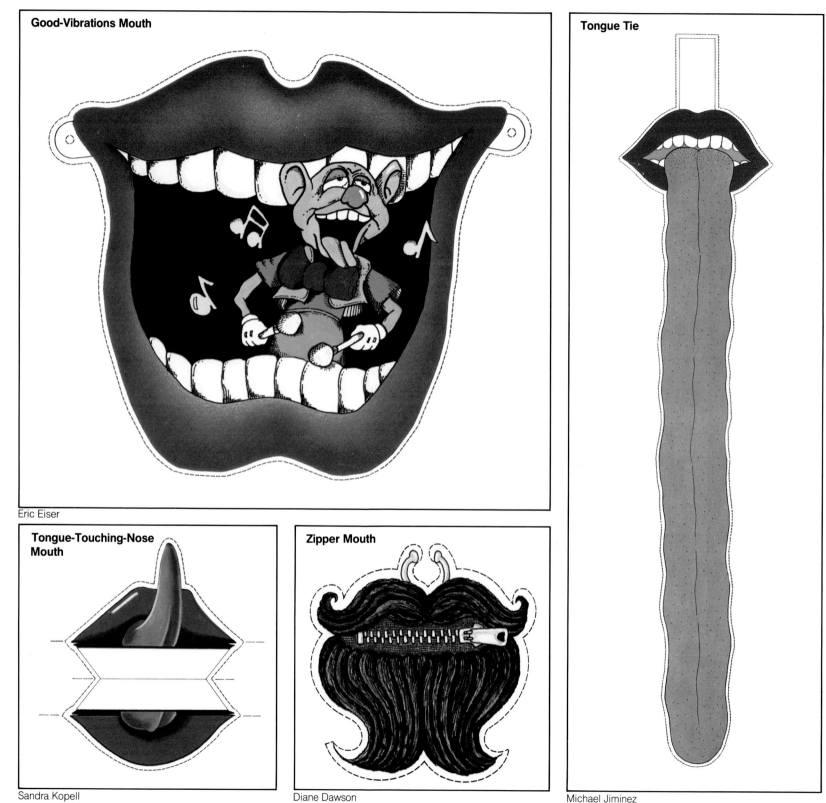

Good-Vibrations Mouth

Eric Eiser

Tongue-Touching-Nose Mouth

Sandra Kopell

Zipper Mouth

Diane Dawson

Tongue Tie

Michael Jiminez

PROBLEM: BODY MASK

SOLUTION:

This assignment is a variation of "Mouth Masks." Again, you are to design a humorous mask, but this time, it is to be used for any part of the body.

SPECIFICATIONS

Size: No restrictions; concept to dictate size and shape.
Color: Full color.
Medium: No limitation.
Requirement: Indicate all perforations, folds, and cutouts

Cauliflower Ear

Joseph Ianelli

Seaman's Moustache

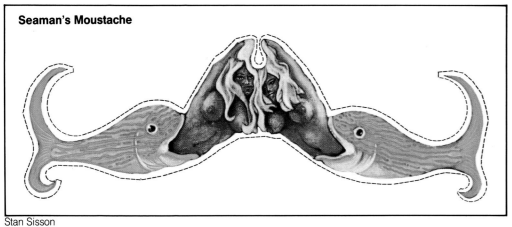

Stan Sisson

Dancing Girls

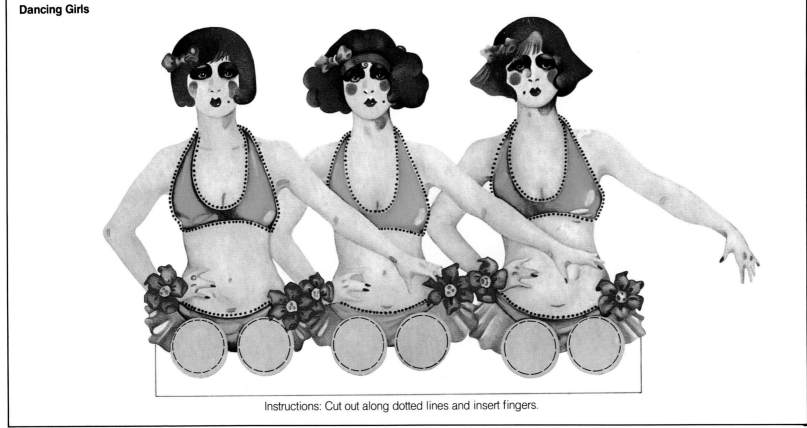

Instructions: Cut out along dotted lines and insert fingers.

Cheryl Griesbach/Stanley Martucci

94

PROBLEM: EYEGLASS MASK

SOLUTION:

This assignment is also a variation of "Mouth Masks." Using the commonplace imagery that usually depicts a city, design a mask in the form of eyeglasses.

SPECIFICATIONS

Size: No restrictions; concept to dictate size and shape.
Color: Full color.
Medium: No limitation.
Requirement: Indicate all perforations, folds, and cutouts.
Note: Any city is acceptable.

Miami Beach

Mark Samuels

New York City

Mark Samuels

Imagery seen too frequently is often not seen at all. This is the case with overused design symbols and everyday objects. Overuse renders them ineffective, and they lose their power to communicate. It is the function of the designer to revitalize these clichéd symbols and objects by interpreting them in individual and personal ways. The following twelve assignments are variations of this problem.

SPECIFICATIONS

Size: 4 by 6 inches.
Color: Black and white.
Medium: No limitation.
Note: In an advanced version of this assignment, a personalized logo using the given cliché is designed.

Logo Design: Michael Delevante

96

Kam Mak

Marilyn Schonhaut

Suzette Desmond

Caroline Mailhot

Martha Kennelly

Cornelia Bremer

Suzette Desmond

■ "Look for the stars, you'll say that there are none..." (Wordsworth) ■ Things which are seen often, stop being seen at all ■ It is the function of a good designer to take a cliche symbol, and by applying a personal sense of style, reinterpret and make it visible once more ■ Based upon an experimental class project at the School of Visual Arts, this poster presents twenty individual interpretations of this familiar American symbol ■

Logo Design: Alain Giguere

Kristin Barnet

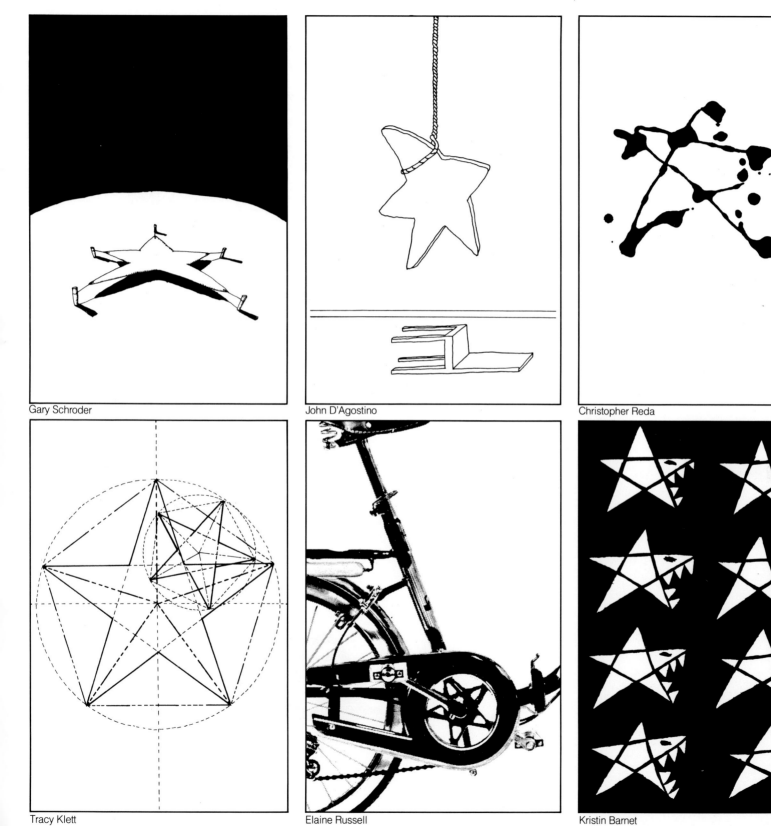

Gary Schroder

John D'Agostino

Christopher Reda

Tracy Klett

Elaine Russell

Kristin Barnet

99

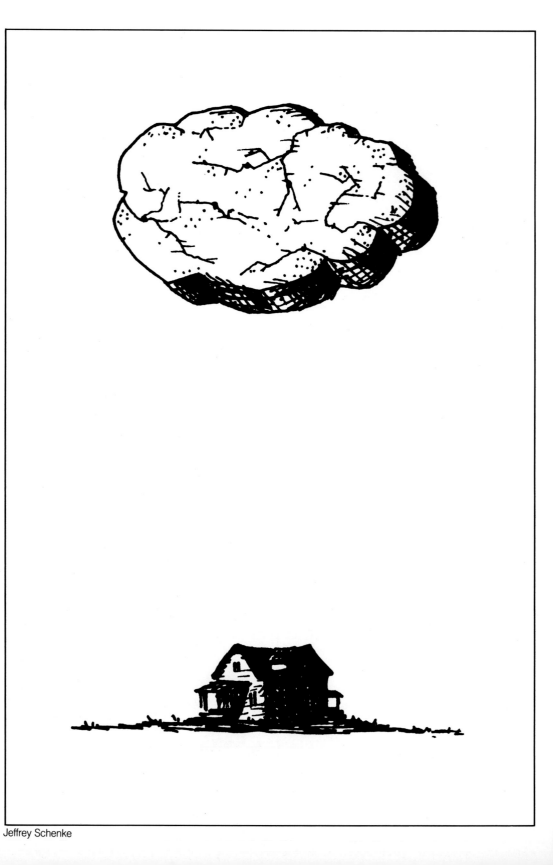

Logo Design: Diane Addesso

Jeffrey Schenke

Carmen Zeif

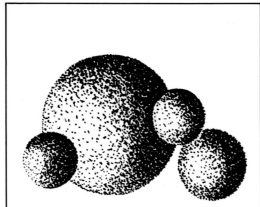

Marie Castellano

Christopher Merola

Wendy Balbo

John Rea

Lesli Schlau

Logo Design: Alexandra Guzak

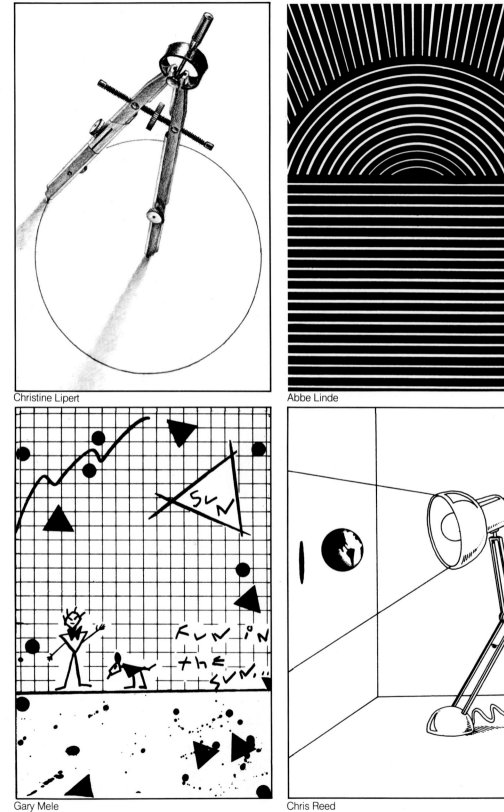

Christine Lipert

Abbe Linde

Gary Mele

Chris Reed

Anne D. Bernstein

Pat Scanlon

Nancy Tuttle

Logo Design: Kathi Rota

Sheryl Cooper

Elaine Woolcock

Robert Santora

Mark Hriciga

Rosa Empis

Scott Wadler

Robert Wallman

APPLES

A is for apple.
You are the apple of my eye.
As American as apple pie
An apple for the teacher.

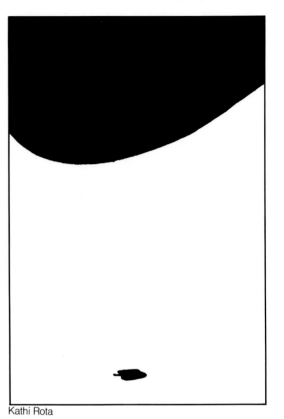

Nadine Badalaty

Kathi Rota

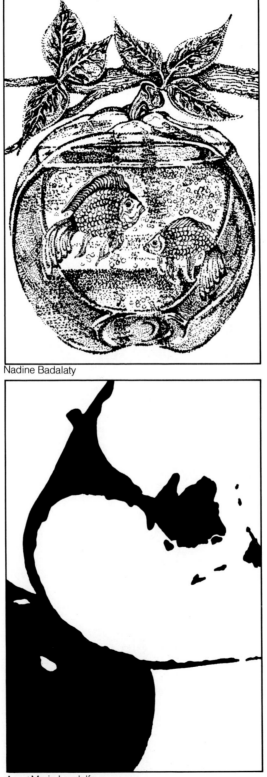

Anna Marie Landolfo

Randi Schiffman

Logo Design: Susan Spivack

Dana Digirolamo

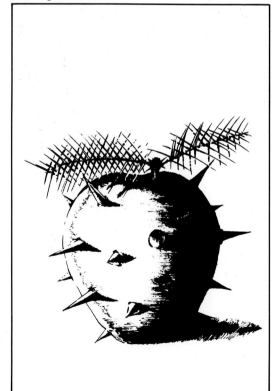

Tom Park

Ellen Feinberg

PROBLEM: KEY

SOLUTION:

Logo Design: Dan Simon   Illustration: Todd Radom

Jareth Holub

Timothy O'Keefe

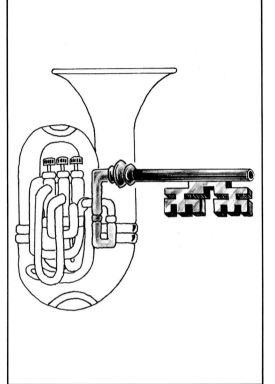

Hyocha Koo

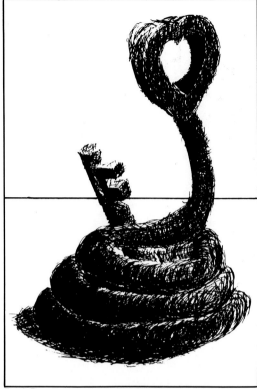

Frank Donote

Anne Reilly

Todd Radom

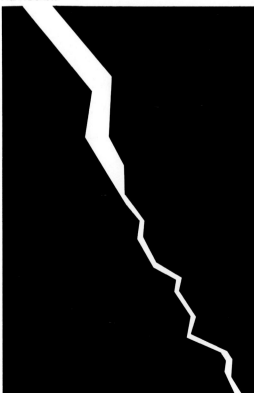

Andrea Santschi

PROBLEM: NUTS AND BOLTS

SOLUTION:

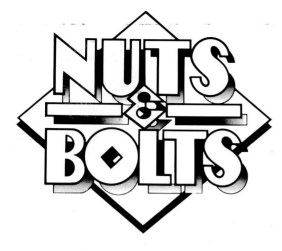

Logo Design: Darryl Ligason

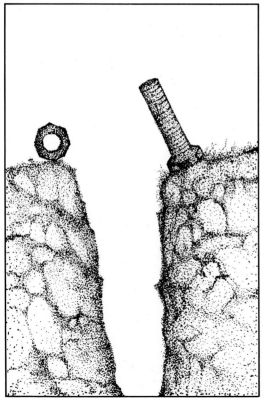

Marc Bailey

Merryl L. Mayer

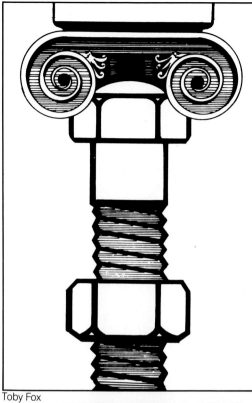

Toby Fox

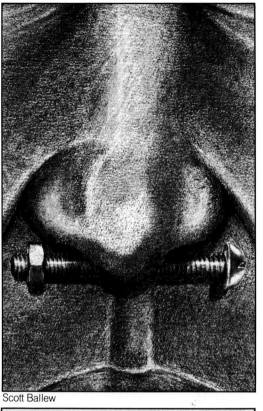

Scott Ballew

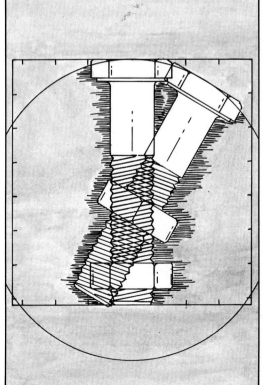

Christine Lee

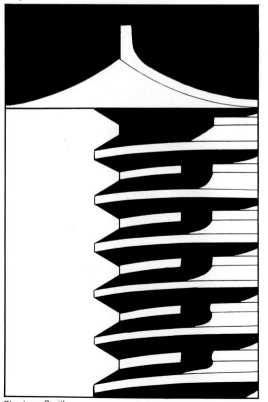

Sharleen Smith

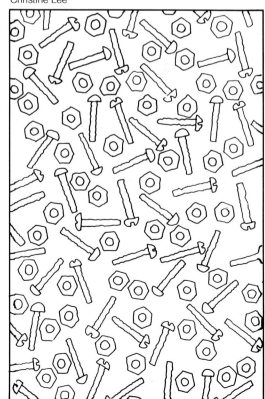

Tom Godici

Althea Loglia

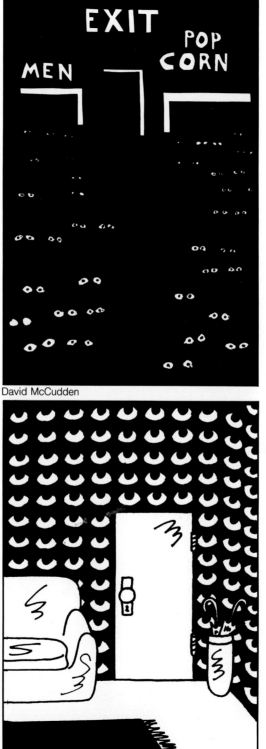

David McCudden

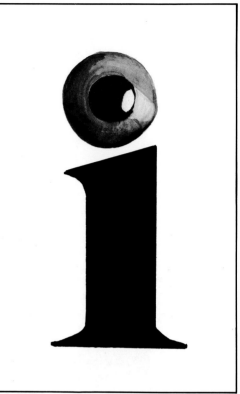

Pamela Maffei

Keith Mastandrea

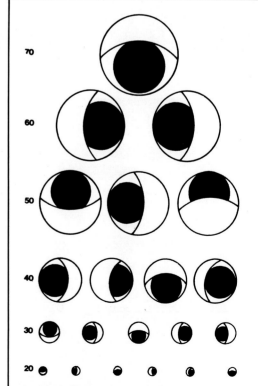

Jeanette D'Ambrosio

Logo Design: Ayelet Bender

Michael Howett

Tammi Colichio

Robert Westhoff

Mariette Steinman

Larry Risko

Barbara Osborne

113

PROBLEM: TREE

SOLUTION:

Logo Design: John Rea

Phil Milano

Donna Epstein

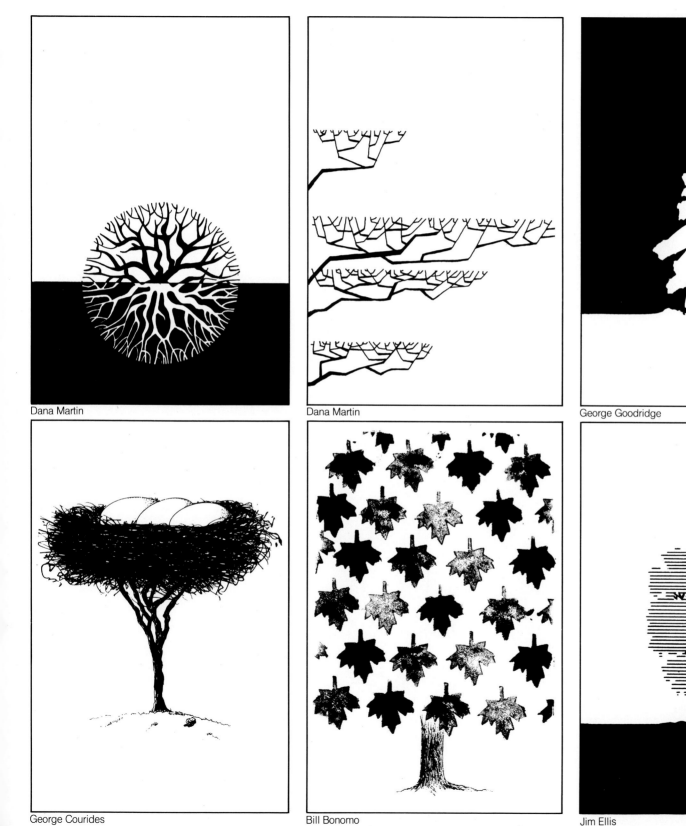

Dana Martin

Dana Martin

George Goodridge

George Courides

Bill Bonomo

Jim Ellis

115

PROBLEM: MOUTH   **SOLUTION:**

Logo Design: Scott Wadler

Juan Caceres

Melanie Lowe

Susan M. Lyons

Paul H. Devejia

Daniel O'Leary

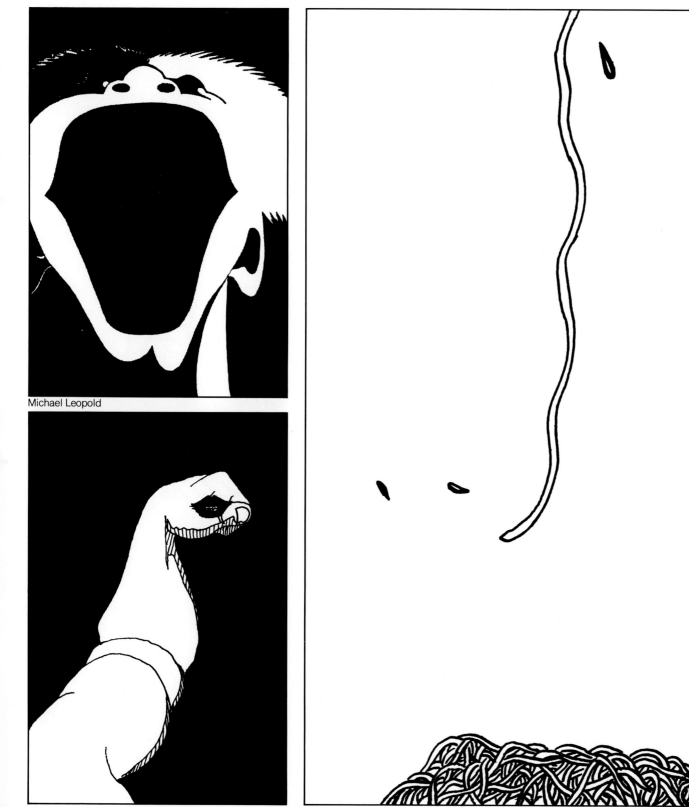

Michael Leopold

Paul Scarsella

Alan Labate

PROBLEM: LIGHT BULB   **SOLUTION:**

Logo Design: Joseph Baron

Nicholas Taylor

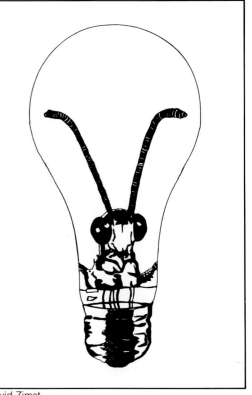

David Zimet

Barbara Cruz

Jerome Boxley

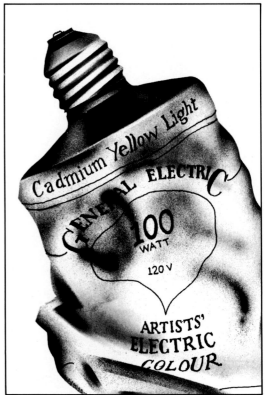

Xavier Wasowski

Xavier Wasowski

Joyce Novotny

Charles Lipscomb

119

Choose a theme or circumstance that recurs in your life. Convey it in a chronological sequence, using no less than nine and no more than fifteen images. The effectiveness and clarity of each of these images can be increased by adding copy that memorably ties into or explains the visual. The technique of copy "paying off" the visual or the visual "paying off" the copy is often used in advertising. The subtle balance between picture and words is crucial in creating an effective message.

SINGLE SOLUTIONS: Each single solution should be able to stand on its own.

SPECIFICATIONS

Size: Each visual must be on a separate panel, 3 by 5 inches each.
Color: Black and white.
Medium: Pen and ink, pencil, or felt-tip markers.
Copy: Include copy to pay off visuals. Include dates to support the chronology. Create a headline for the entire assignment. A subheading is optional.

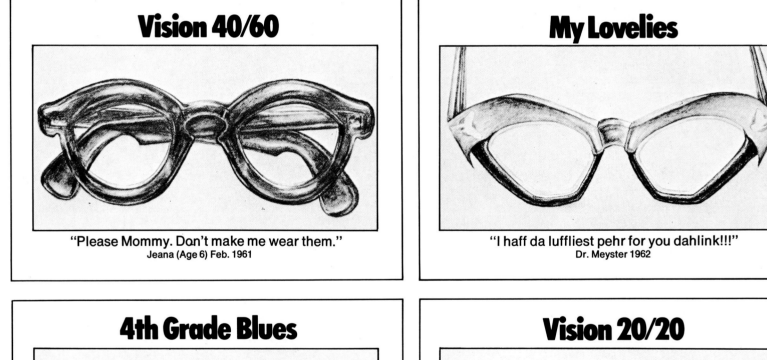

Vision 40/60

"Please Mommy. Don't make me wear them."
Jeana (Age 6) Feb. 1961

My Lovelies

"I haff da luffliest pehr for you dahlink!!!"
Dr. Meyster 1962

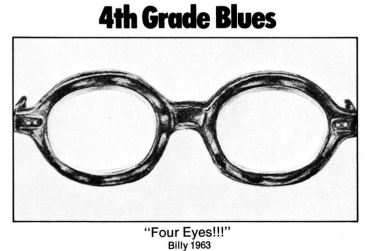

4th Grade Blues

"Four Eyes!!!"
Billy 1963

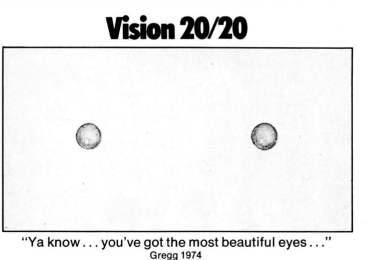

Vision 20/20

"Ya know . . . you've got the most beautiful eyes . . ."
Gregg 1974

Glasses

A Self-Portrait / Jeana Sirabella

Vision 40/60

"Please Mommy. Don't make me wear them."
Jeana (Age 6) Feb. 1961

Vision 40/200

"Stop squinting and put on your DAMN glasses!"
Dad Oct. 1961

My Lovelies

"I haff da luffliest pehr for you dahlink!!!"
Dr. Meyster 1962

4th Grade Blues

"Four Eyes!!!"
Billy 1963

5th Grade Blues

"Can you see the blackboard back there?!"
Mrs. Rosen 1964

Eye Spy

"Are you looking at me?"
Jeana March 1966

Jeana Jock

"What are ya Blind!? He was out by a mile!"
Corky & Danny Aug. 1966

Jeana Lolita

"Hey, Jeana's got a nice pair, huh? ha . . . ha . . . ha . . ."
Dougie (he wanted me) Rizzo 1967

Jeana Shrimpton

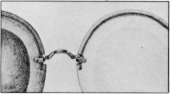

"So Jean Shrimpton has a pointy nose, So?"
Jeana 1967

Tuff

"I wonder if they'll recognize me."
Jeana 1969

Jeana Cycle

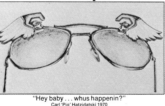

"Hey baby . . . whus happenin?"
Carl 'Pig' Hatzidatski 1970

Bus Driver

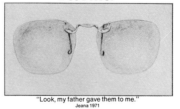

"Look, my father gave them to me."
Jeana 1971

Jeana Hooker

"Catch-this . . . innocent Jeana on the make!!"
Paul Koehler to Nina Donnelly 1972

Gloria Steinem Compromise

"JEANA! YOU'RE not wearing a BRA?!"
Robin Wolin 1973

Vision 20/20

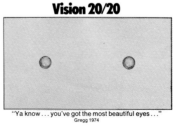

"Ya know . . . you've got the most beautiful eyes . . ."
Gregg 1974

The School of Visual Arts

Student Experimental Program · Media Arts Department
209 East 23rd Street, New York, New York 10010 (212) 679-7350

Jeana Sirabella

SOLUTION:

SINGLE SOLUTIONS: Each single solution should
be able to stand on its own.

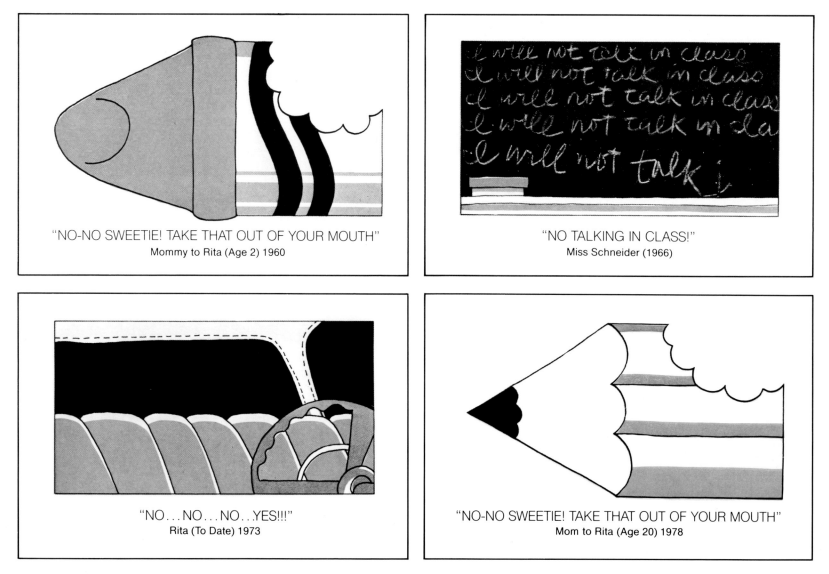

"NO-NO SWEETIE! TAKE THAT OUT OF YOUR MOUTH"
Mommy to Rita (Age 2) 1960

"NO TALKING IN CLASS!"
Miss Schneider (1966)

"NO...NO...NO...YES!!!"
Rita (To Date) 1973

"NO-NO SWEETIE! TAKE THAT OUT OF YOUR MOUTH"
Mom to Rita (Age 20) 1978

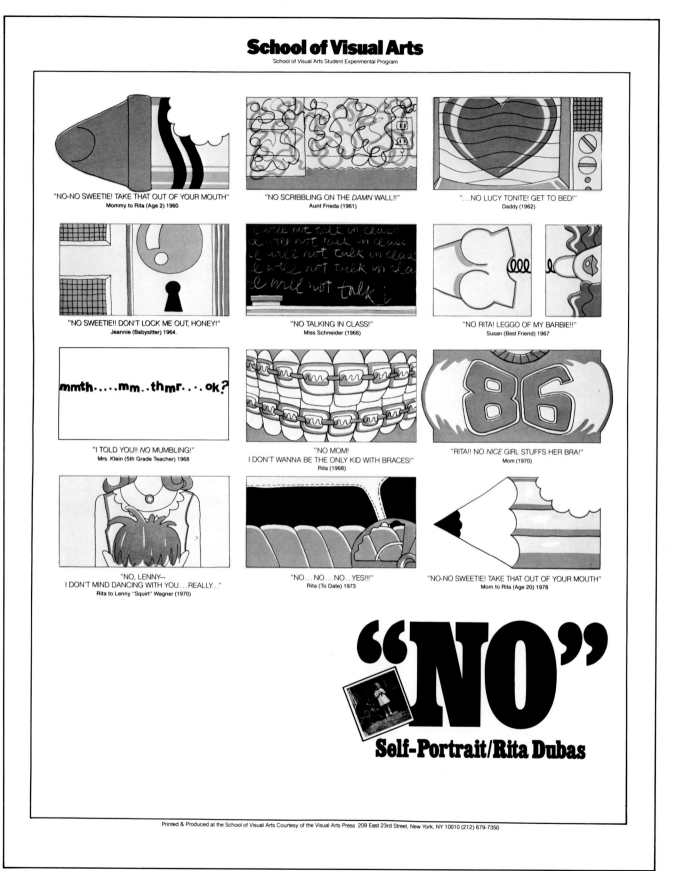

Rita Dubas

Printed & Produced at the School of Visual Arts Courtesy of the Visual Arts Press 209 East 23rd Street, New York, NY 10010 (212) 679-7350

PROBLEM: PIN THE _____ ON THE _____

Pin the tail on the donkey is a popular children's game. The special quality of the game lies in the excitement of having to complete something that cannot be seen: will the tail end up in its proper place, or will it be in some odd place, creating a humorous result? The game is a success because it relies on the visual excitement of the unexpected.

You can change your perception of the familiar by personalizing it. Choose any topic that interests you and design it in the form of pin the tail on the donkey.

When you use a familiar form, such as pin the tail on the donkey, as a means of solving a design problem, you must extend and personally interpret the form to communicate effectively. Otherwise, your solution becomes mere imitation, with no power.

SPECIFICATIONS

Size: 24 by 18 inches.
Color: Full color or black and white.
Medium: No limitation.
Copy: Title must be included.

Pin the Beef on the Bumper

Steve Hodowsky

Pin the Smokestack on the New Jersey Skyline

Jeff Faust

SOLUTION:

Pin the Next Animal on the Extinction List

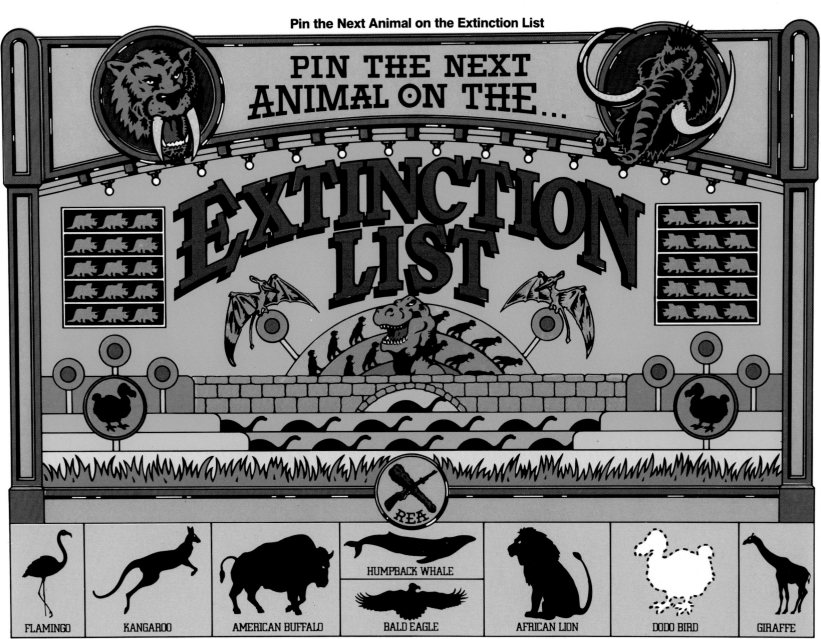

125

PART 2. EXHIBITIONS AS A MEANS FOR PROBLEM SOLVING

Each of the following problems was organized around an original theme that encompassed a wide range of possible solutions. Students in a variety of visual communication areas—graphic design, illustration, advertising, and cartooning, for example—could all work on the same theme, even though their skills differed.

Each project was considered as the basis for an exhibition focusing on the stated theme. A jury of instructors selected the best pieces of artwork. To extend the design experience, design students and instructors worked together to create promotional material, such as posters, catalogs, invitations, and advertisements, which in turn became the basis for creating an identity for the exhibition.

A juried exhibition based on an original concept in which the best pieces become printed samples creates a competitive spirit among students. This competition can help students extend themselves beyond their perceived limitations. It also teaches students ultimately to compete against themselves in an effort toward self-improvement.

PROBLEM: MASKS: COME OUT, COME OUT, WHOEVER YOU ARE

SOLUTION:

What are the psychological masks or images we use to hide behind, the postures we use to present ourselves to others in everyday life? In one form or another, we all hide behind images of ourselves, which may take the form of clothing, facial expressions, hairstyles, speech, and the like. Often your most closely guarded secret is a secret many others hide as well. So dare to look at yourself objectively and expose a personal truth in the form of a mask that describes an emotion, attitude, habit, or overall posture that you hide behind. The mask should be three-dimensional.

SPECIFICATIONS

Size: Approximately life size.
Color: Any colors.
Medium: No limitation.
Copy: Title and explain your mask in a short paragraph on its reverse side.

GRANDFATHER MASK

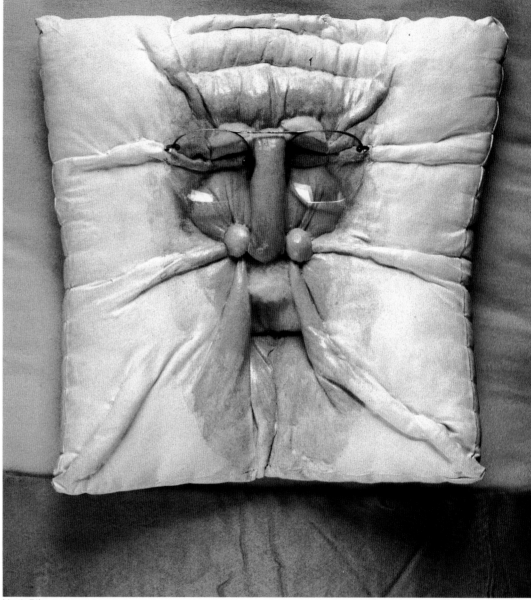

Hugh Biber

HORROR MASK

Cynthia Emidio

QUOTES FROM "RELIABLE" SOURCES

Laura Goodman

PLAIN BROWN BAG

Joseph Malone

129

SOLUTION:

HEAD IN THE CLOUDS

Mary Citarella

SHE THE MOUNTAIN

Susan Grillo

A VESTIGE

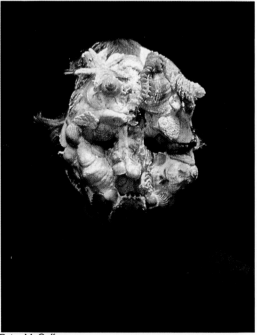

Peter McCaffrey

IMPOSSIBLE SEXUALITY

Peter Ranalli

VENUS

Tammy Sweet

THE BACKSTABBER

Pam Fogel

A BRICK FACADE

Susan Spivack

THE GRIM JESTER

Sharon Tondreau

TRANSPARENT AS GLASS

Amy Gruenwald

A FLY IN THE OINTMENT

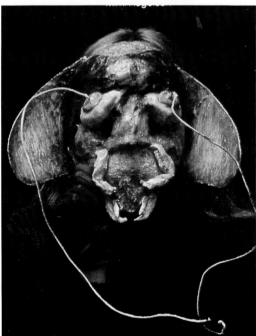

Mimi Regelson

SOLUTION:

MY STRAIGHT FACE

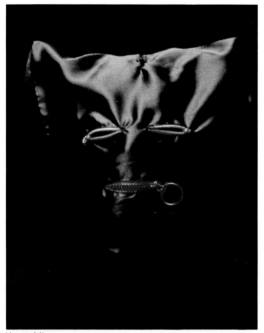

Karen Minster

THE THORN AND THE ROSE

Sydney Campbell

OPEN AND CLOSE AT WILL

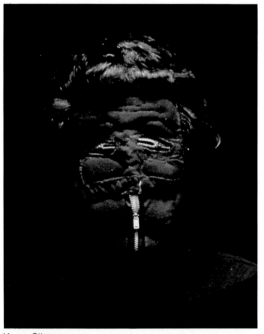

Karen Silver

THE "SERIOUS" ARTIST

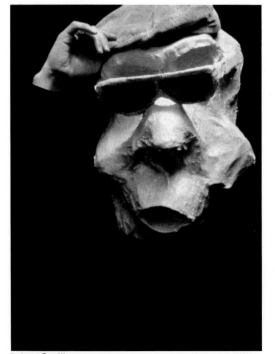

Robert Casilla

FANCY SCHMANCY

Rita Dubas

SOFT BUT IMPENETRABLE FOG

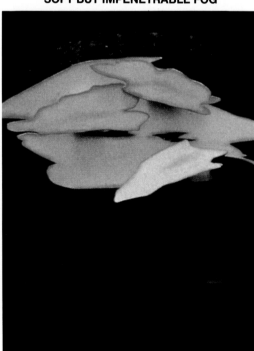

Laura Freeman

PROBLEM: MASKS: POSTER

Select and combine various solutions from the masks submitted to create a single graphic image that suggests the wide scope of this assignment.

SPECIFICATIONS

Size: 20 by 32 inches.
Color: Four-color process.
Stock: Gloss-coated text.
Copy: Include a brief description and title for each mask.
Printing: Offset lithography.

MASK DESCRIPTIONS:

TOP:
Isn't it strange that a mask—made to be frightening—is also afraid? Often I am intimidated by others only to find that, underneath, they live in fear as much as I do.
—Nancy Ward

MIDDLE:
My mask is all the false fatness that thin people like me pretend to have. By talking about my "weight problem," I get everyone else to assure me that I'm thin!
—Laura Goodman

BOTTOM:
My mask, constructed of bricks, looks solid and strong. But in reality it's just a façade of strength; a mask of pretense, protecting and concealing interior weakness.
—Susan Spivack

Nancy Ward, Laura Goodman, and Susan Spivack

Design or illustrate a used car that you would like to sell. You can make direct reference to any car model. Your car may be:

a. Real—based on stories you have heard or on your own experience.
b. Fantasy—the used car of the twenty-first century.
c. Based on a personality—the last car owned by a celebrity. Show whose car it was by altering the surface or structure of the car.
d. Based on a stereotype—the last car owned by a drug dealer, a Texas oilman, or a New York City taxi driver.
e. Based on a phenomenon or event—a car being sold after exposure to acid rain or after an accident in an automatic car wash.

Attach an advertisement of the car to the artwork. Write the ad in abbreviated language, as it would appear in a newspaper's classified section. Remember that used cars generally have bad reputations. Experiment with the idea of contradiction between what you say the car is like and what it really looks like. Exaggerate. Consider oddities: stretch limousines, jeeps, dune buggies, snowmobiles, trucks, vans, and hybrids. In fact, the only inflexible criterion in this assignment is that, however you deal with the car in your artwork, in part or as a whole, with other objects or by itself, what you show must be identifiable as a car.

SPECIFICATIONS

Size: 18 by 18 inches maximum.
Three-dimensional solutions:
18 by 18 by 18 inches maximum.
Color: Full color or black and white.
Medium: No limitation.
Copy: Write a description of the car for sale in classified-ad jargon.

1. Frank Collado

2. Fred Castelluccio

1. For sale: Vintage 1937 Packard. Remarkably FRESH paint job. Body completely smooth. A JUICY offer you can't pass up. Call Orchard Autos: 555–7126.

2. Completely restored 1920s 2-door COOP. Custom exterior. Original owner nationally known chicken farmer. This car is no gas hog, costs chicken feed to run. Price negotiable or will trade for golden egg. Call: 555–0500. Ask for Frank.

3. For sale: Slim-line, 5-speed, fully loaded, rust-proofed, a/c, country-driven sedan. Must see. Owner deceased for 35 years. Car hardly driven.

4. Honest Al's used car lot. Must see. All cars have original bodies. Any one a real PEACH of a buy. Come on down and pick one or call: 555–PEEL.

3. Kye Baker

4. Frank Gargiulo

SOLUTION:

5. Transit Authority official wants to sell Cadillac limo w/power windows/doors. Customized paint job and body work.

6. Is the used car game DRIVING you crazy? Feel like you never get a BRAKE? Are dealers STEERING you wrong? If you don't play your cards right, DEPRECIATION will make your repair bills soar and leave you in debt. Play the used car game with pros. Do not pass GO, come directly to Boardgame Motors, Chance, Long Island, N.Y.

5. John C. Ward, Jr.

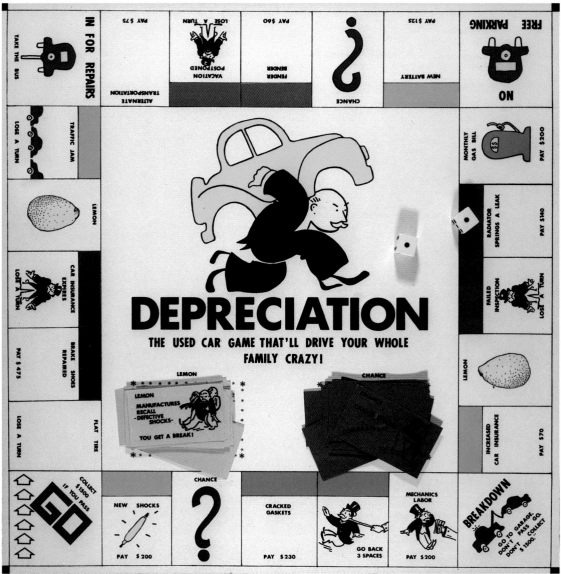

6. Charles McGill

7. Ernest Albanese

7. Vintage 1917 Mercedes, modified specially by owner driving in heavy traffic. Blue Max Motors: 555–7247, ask for Baron von Richtoven.

8. Used '75 Ford Pinto. Extensive safety modifications added by previous owner.

8. Philip Travisano

SOLUTION:

9. For sale at astonishingly low price. 1928 Packard. Matchless appeal. Specially built, light boxy exterior complements compact interior.

10. Corvette, 1961 B.C. Perfectly preserved. For immediate purchase. Driven only on special occasions by owner's mummy. Call: 555–1222, ask for Tut or Isis.

11. Must sell classic silver gray coupe. Property of a lady. Monumentally well cared for. Statuesque lines. Solid grillework.

12. Used car for sale. Mint condition parts. Some assembly required.

9. Thomas Sciacca

10. Fran Reckson

11. Lorenzo Cardi

12. Rebecca Duke

SOLUTION:

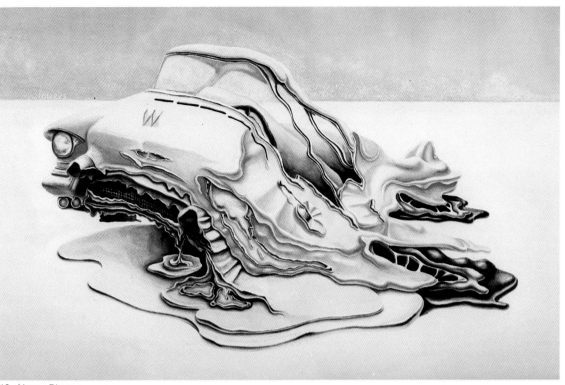

13. Nancy Blowers

14. James Sullivan

13. Used 1957 Cadillac Coupe de Ville. Smooth, flowing lines. Only driven short distance to work by former director of nuclear power plant.

14. Bentley '36 classic carefully pieced together. Some assembly still required.

15. For sale: '39 Plymouth, mint interior. Unusual 2-tone paint job. (212) 555–4754.

16. Sale. Used custom convertible w/5-speed glide ride makes traveling a pleasure.

15. David Dircks

16. Michael Morshuk

SOLUTION:

17. Richard Rehbin

17. Customized traffic buster beats New York City car crunch! Excellent visibility from driver's seat. For sale by retiring commuter.

18. Ride high in your own little VW convertible! Great on gas. Excellent for car owner on a budget. Fully automatic. Practically drives itself. Don't be taken for a joy ride on those other used car deals!

18. Stuart Koban

PROBLEM: USED CARS FOR SALE: CATALOG

Exaggerating the truth can effectively communicate a concept. Using this idea as a point of departure, create a catalog cover for the exhibition "Used Cars for Sale."

SPECIFICATIONS

Size: 8 by 11 inches.
Color: Four-color process.
Stock: Gloss-coated cover weight.
Printing: Offset lithography.

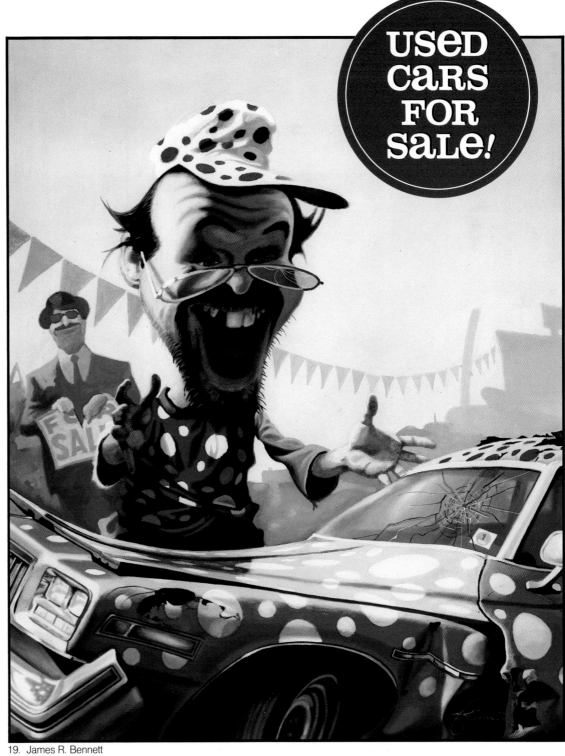

19. James R. Bennett

Graphically depict an object from our decade that could become an artifact in 100 years. Choose an object that says so much about the 1980s that an archeologist could some day dig it up and classify it as circa 1985. Assuming our culture changes as dramatically in the next 100 years as it has in the last, what do you think these objects would imply about us to the people living in 2085?

When discovered, your artifact can still be in perfect condition or it can be petrified, decayed, cracked, or in some other way marked by time. It may be that only a fragment of the artifact is found. However much or little of the artifact you visualize, what it represents must be clear and symbolic of contemporary culture.

SPECIFICATIONS

Size: 18 by 24 inches maximum.
Three-dimensional solutions:
18 by 18 by 18 inches maximum.
Color: Full color or black and white.
Medium: No limitation.

SOLUTION:

Susan Barrasi

Grace Gepfert

Ernest Albanese

William Ferguson

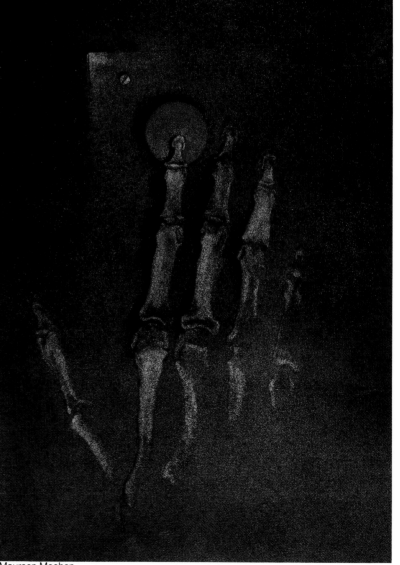

Maureen Meehan

145

Fayge Silverman

Dennis Glock

MADE IN JAPAN

Lorenzo Cardi

James Bennett

Maria Jimenez

SOLUTION:

Floyd M. Rappy

Lorne Lanning

John C. Ward, Jr.

Luis Vasquez

148

Mark Anthony

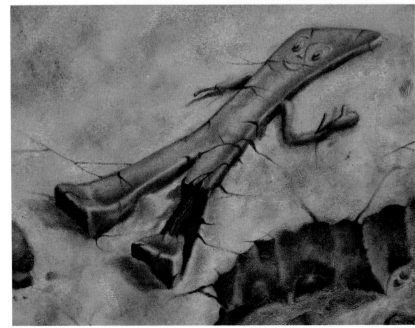

Edward Heck

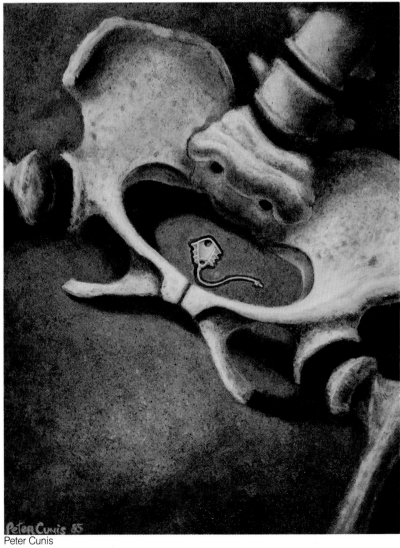

Peter Cunis

SOLUTION:

Ted Sokolowski

Sue Sullenberger

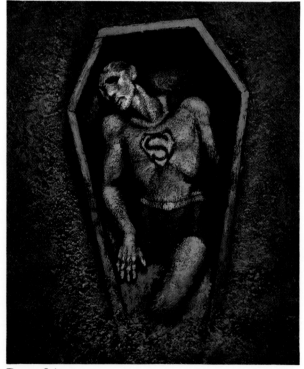

Thomas Sciacca

150

PROBLEM: ARTIFACTS: PROMOTION

Design a poster and invitation for the exhibition "Artifacts: What Will Survive?" with a logotype to be used on all promotional material. The logotype should create an identity for the exhibition.

SPECIFICATIONS: POSTER

Size: 22 by 31 inches.
Color: Four-color process.
Stock: Gloss-coated text.
Printing: Offset lithography.

SPECIFICATIONS: INVITATION

Size: 5¼ by 7¼ inches.
Color: Four-color process.
Stock: Gloss-coated cover weight.
Printing: Offset lithography.

The Media Arts Department of the School of
Visual Arts cordially invites you to the opening of
its annual exhibition on
Thursday, May 2, 1985, from 5:00-8:00 P.M.
at the Master Eagle Gallery, sixth floor,
40 West 25th Street, New York, New York.

Illustrator: **Paul Cozzolino**

Paul Cozzolino

Fred Castelluccio

<151>151</151>

PROBLEM: A MATTER OF LIFE AND DEATH   **SOLUTION:**

This theme encompasses a problem to be solved in two parts. Part one must accurately represent any subject (animal, vegetable, mineral). Part two should show its death or destruction. Solutions may involve any subject matter as long as the two separate conditions of life and death are clear.

The life/death images may be literal or abstract: in death an ice cube becomes a small puddle of water; in death, the color green separates into blue and yellow. It is also possible to reverse the problem and show that the death of one thing results in the life of another, that things die so others can come into existence.

Before beginning work on any one idea, you might make a list of fifty or so life/death images. Start with obvious ideas and expand. This may be useful in helping to define your ideas.

SPECIFICATIONS

Size: 14 by 17 inches maximum.
Three-dimensional solutions:
2 by 2 by 2 feet maximum.
Color: Full color or black and white.
Medium: No limitation.
Requirement: All solutions must consist of two separate panels of equal size.

Scott Frommer

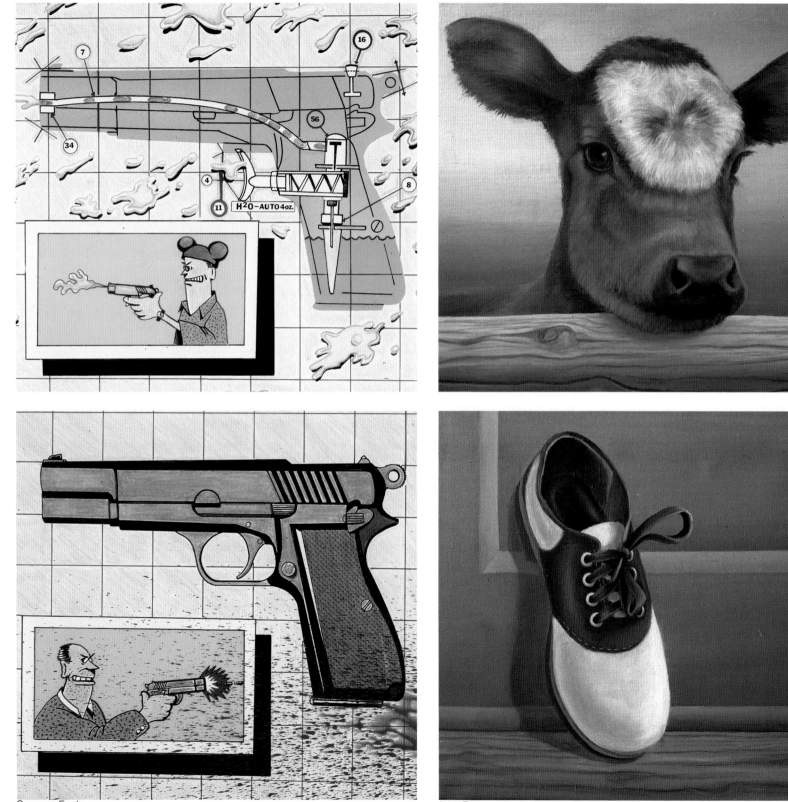

Cameron Eagle

Anne Pace

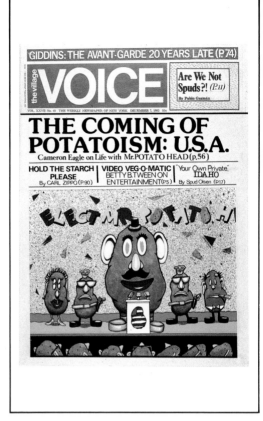

WHEN DEATH KNOCKS ON YOUR DOOR, GREET IT WITH ETERNAL LIFE...

TODAYS TAXIDERMIST SPECIAL "IN FLIGHT"

Cameron Eagle

Chris Reed

154

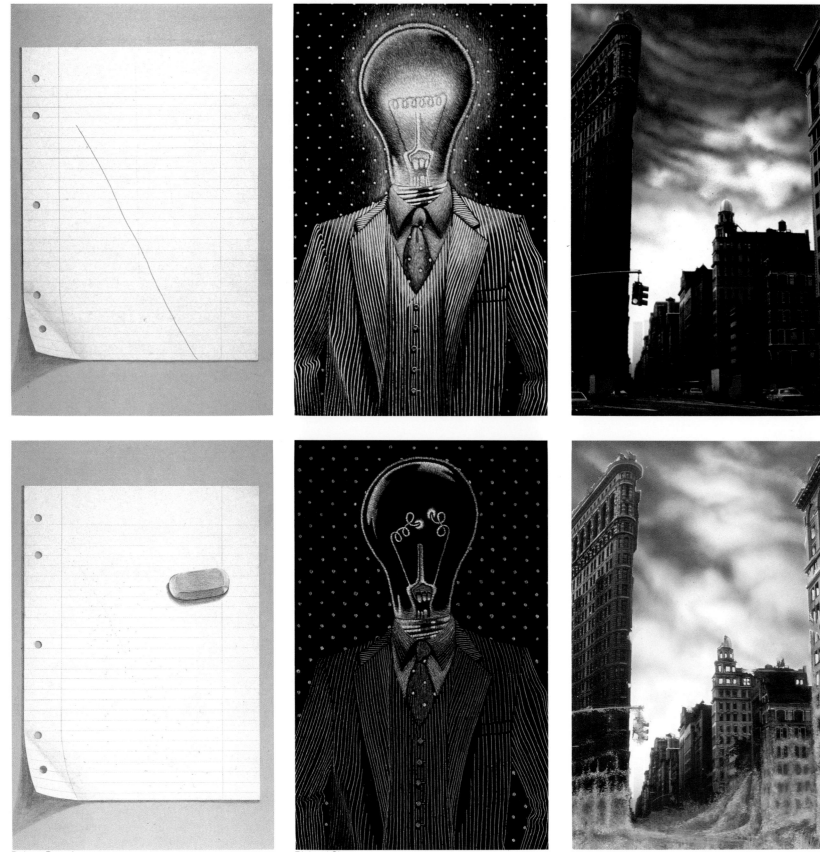

Delmar Demelo

Richard Sierra

Unknown

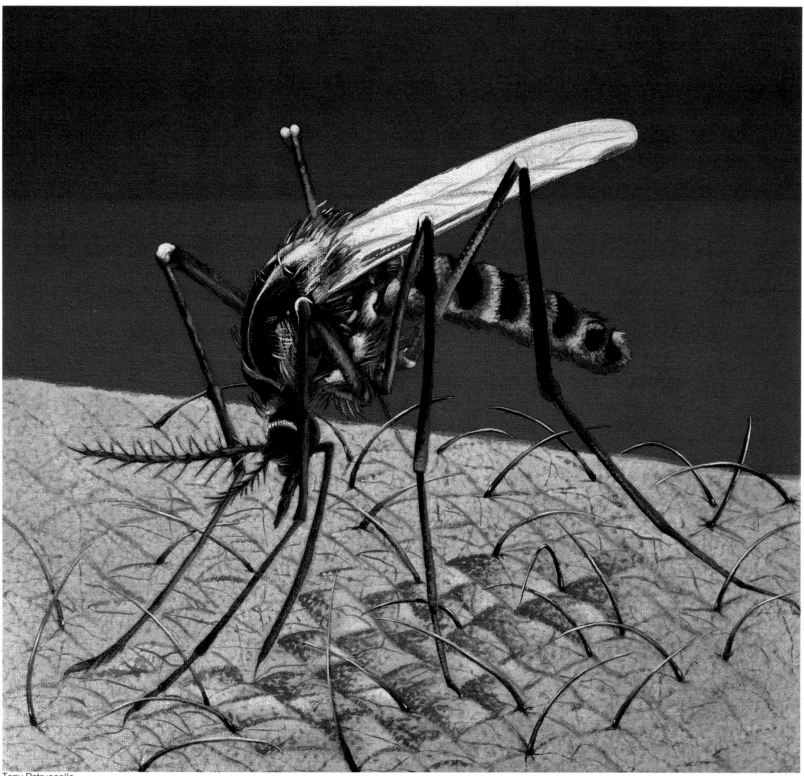

Tony Petruccello

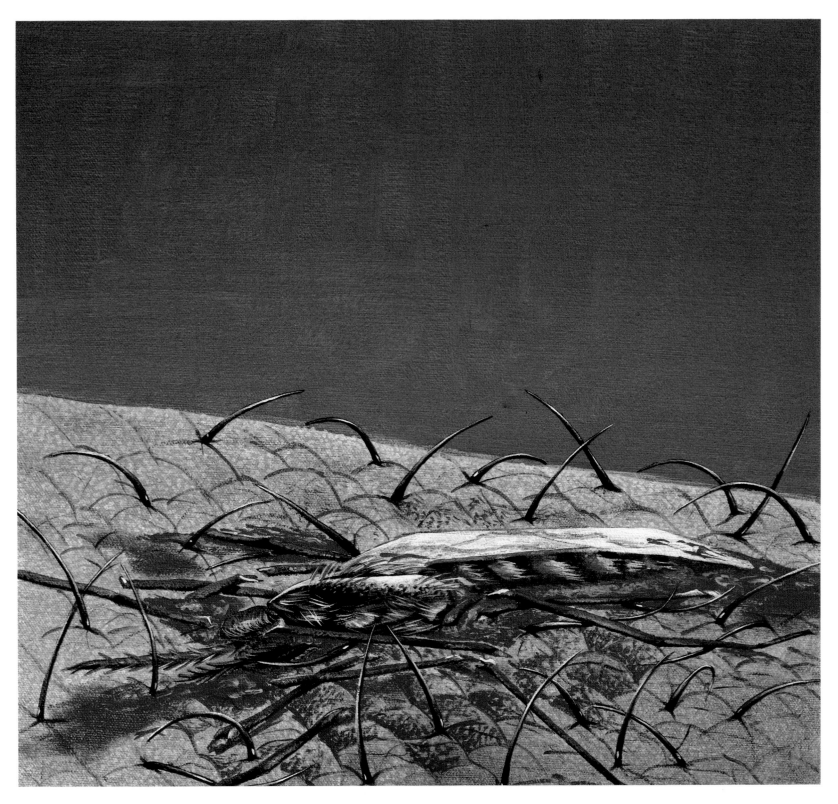

157

SOLUTIONS:

Vincent Nasta

Mickey Paraskevas

158

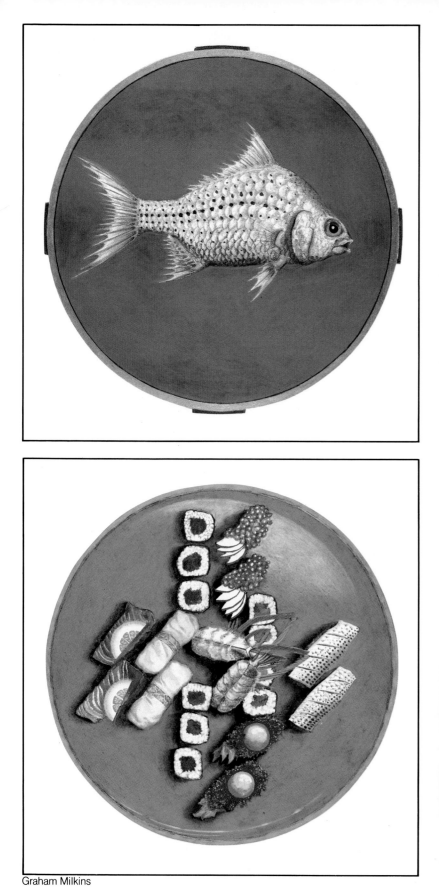

Graham Milkins

Darryl Zudek

159

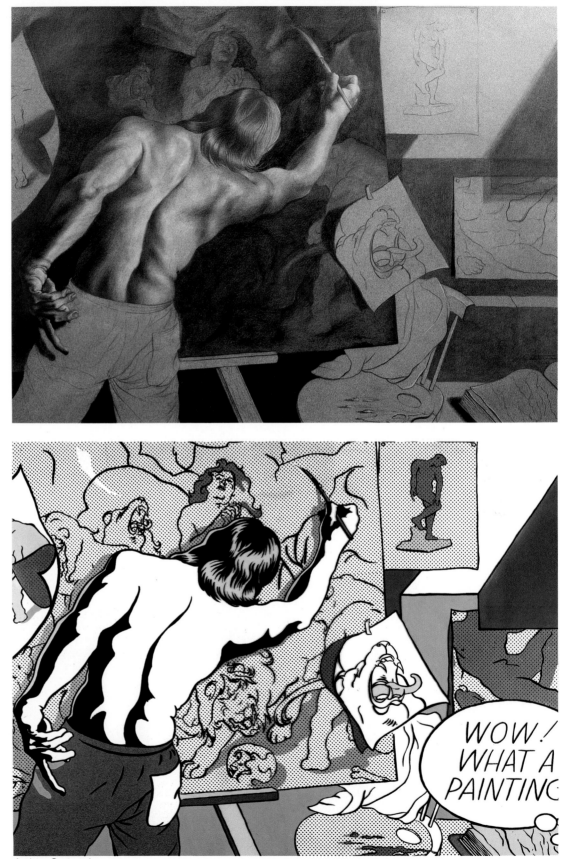

Andrew Castrucci

PROBLEM: A MATTER OF LIFE AND DEATH:
POSTER

Using a two-panel format, create a poster that expresses the concept "A Matter of Life and Death" and also conveys the range of the assignment.

SPECIFICATIONS

Size: 33 by 21 inches.
Color: Four-color process.
Stock: Gloss-coated text.
Limitation: The two panels must be of equal size.
Printing: Offset lithography.

SOLUTION:

Life and death touch everything. Places, ideas, emotions, events, favorite sneakers and even Coke' cans may all be said to have a life and death. Students in the Media Arts Department at the School of Visual Arts were asked to express this concept in any example of life and death in two separate images. You are cordially invited to see "A Matter of Life and Death," an exhibition of works of personal perspective on this subject. March 26 through May 20, 1983, Master Eagle Gallery, 40 W. 25 Street, 6th floor, 9:00 a.m.- 4:30 p.m., Monday to Friday.

School of Visual Arts
SCHOOL OF VISUAL ARTS IN COOPERATION WITH THE MASTER EAGLE FAMILY OF COMPANIES

Paul Yalowitz

PROBLEM: A MATTER OF LIFE AND DEATH:
VARIATION 1

Convey life and death by combining the two concepts into a single image. *(Shown on this page.)*

SPECIFICATIONS

Size: 14 by 17 inches maximum.
Three-dimensional solutions:
2 by 2 by 2 feet maximum.
Color: Full color or black and white.
Medium: No limitation.

PROBLEM: A MATTER OF LIFE AND DEATH:
VARIATION 2

In three panels, depict life and death using a metamorphic sequence, showing life, death, and the transformation from life to death. With the addition of the third panel, the element of sequence becomes an important aspect of this assignment. *(Shown on facing page.)*

SPECIFICATIONS

Size: 14 by 17 inches maximum.
Three-dimensional solutions:
2 by 2 by 2 feet maximum.
Color: Full color or black and white.
Medium: No limitation.

Susan Diehl

Andrew Castrucci

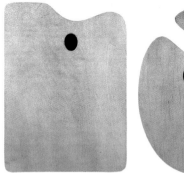

By definition, a palette is a board on which an artist mixes paint. But as a symbol, it has come to stand for the art process and for the artist himself, someone who is unique, isolated, and visionary. The palette as symbol has a romantic quality. Because of the startling transformation in the nature of what is considered art in the twentieth century, the palette now seems quaint and outdated, symbolizing a personality and a process that is appealing but no longer possible in the context of our fast-paced multimedia culture.

Within the confines of the traditional palette, either rectangular or oval shaped, transform the palette into a portrait that reflects the essential characteristics of any chosen individual. Subjects may range from well-known personalities to commonplace stereotypes.

The limitation of the palette shape adds a playful element of challenge to the ancient problem of creating a portrait.

SPECIFICATIONS

Size: As provided.
Color: Full color or black and white.
Medium: No limitation.
Limitation: All work must appear on an oval- or rectangular-shaped palette.
Note: The material aspect of the palette may be changed by reconstructing it out of steel, glass, fabric, or other materials.
Copy: Title your solution.

John J. Audubon

Laurie Baach

164

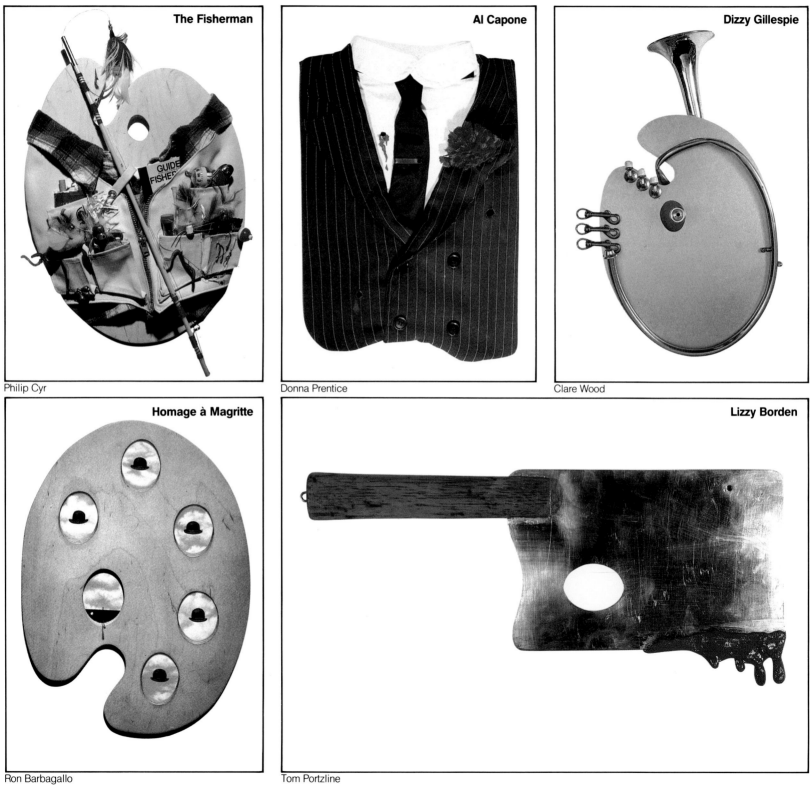

The Fisherman

Philip Cyr

Al Capone

Donna Prentice

Dizzy Gillespie

Clare Wood

Homage à Magritte

Ron Barbagallo

Lizzy Borden

Tom Portzline

Alexander Calder

Jane Tarallo

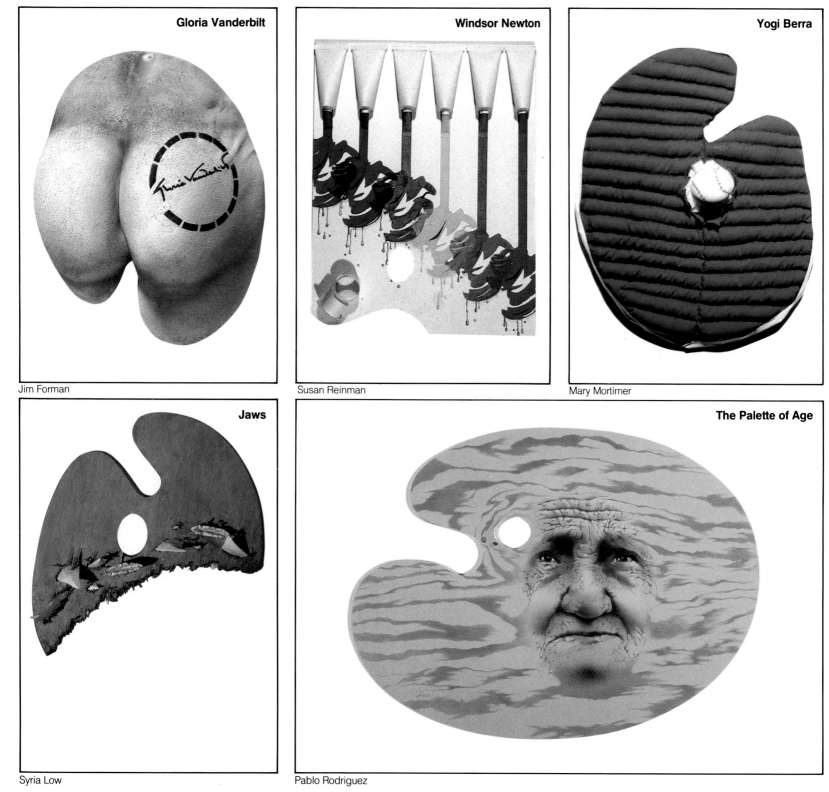

Gloria Vanderbilt

Jim Forman

Windsor Newton

Susan Reinman

Yogi Berra

Mary Mortimer

Jaws

Syria Low

The Palette of Age

Pablo Rodriguez

167

SOLUTION:

The American Housewife

René Magritte

Paul Pullara

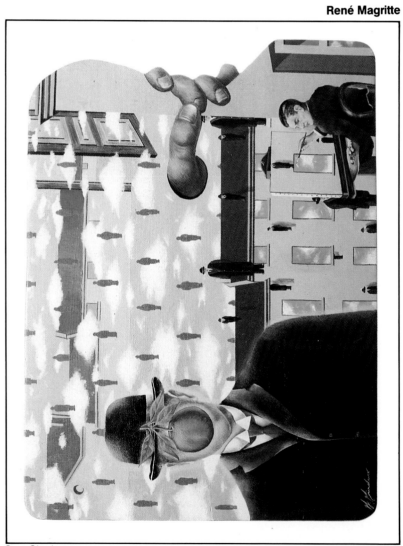

Greg Giordano

After examining the various palette solutions, create a poster to convey the concept of "Homage to the Palette." Because this work will be exhibited in Japan, use a bilingual headline. (Students had access to a Japanese translator.)

SPECIFICATIONS

Size: 28 by 22 inches.
Color: Four-color process.
Stock: Gloss-coated text.
Printing: Offset lithography.

Tom Mennillo, Sean O'Conner, Isaac Kerlow, Michael Grieco, Rita Dubas, Laura Goodman, Bill Donnelly, and Mark J. Tocchet

PROBLEM: APARTMENTS FOR RENT

SOLUTION:

Finding an apartment in New York City has become an epic task. Stories of how difficult this search for space has become range in entertainment value from the bizarre to the ridiculous, from ludicrous to frightening. The disturbing fact seems to be that decent, affordable apartment space in New York City is simply not available.

Depict your most elaborate fantasies or worst nightmares about an available apartment in New York City. Write an accompanying newspaper ad describing it to a prospective tenant. You should depict only one room in the space being rented (even if your proposed apartment has more than one room), then use appropriate newspaper ad jargon to augment your visual.

SPECIFICATIONS

Size: 14 by 14 inches maximum.
Three-dimensional solutions:
14 by 14 by 14 inches maximum.
Color: Full color or black and white.
Medium: No limitation.
Copy: Write a description of the apartment for rent in classified-ad jargon.

1. COMMUTERS share sm studio s/sleeperette. BTHRM AND DINING PRIVL. super conv't to LIRR. perf for man-on-the-go. opn hse Mon-Fri 11:36–11:42 A.M. . . . Grnd Cntrl Station.

2. Apartment for rent—lite, airy 1 bdrm apt. UNOB-STRUCTED VU. quiet residential neighborhood . . . 555–8863.

3. To share with devoted psychiatrist, amazing West Village apartment. 2 bedrooms, spacious, hard to disturb one another, $895.00 a month. Call 555–0123.

4. Apartment for rent with unusually beautiful view! Call 555–0500.

5. Exclusive offer: Beautiful Bensonhurst old-world brownstone furnished in original decor. Original wooden floors and doors. Formerly rented by bus driver and wife, a real steal at only $1500 a month. 555–5818.

6. Room for rent, one and a half bathrooms. Call Wk nites 555–0020.

1. Kymm Ellen Malatesta

2. Maria Jimenez

3. Lynn Pieroni

5. Todd Radom

4. James R. Jennings

6. Diane Merkel

SOLUTION:

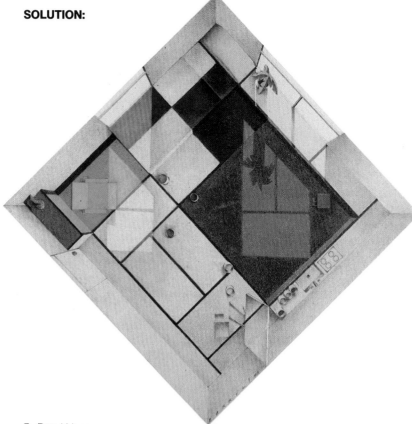

7. Darryl Ligasan

9. Philip Travisano

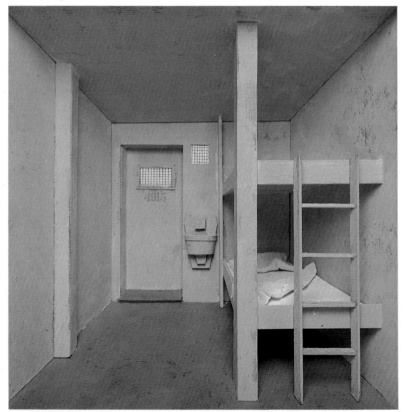

8. Luca Mazzola

10. David Dircks

7. Room for Rent—semi-furn, colorful, MODERN DECOR. former artists studio. Call weekends 555–3250

8. Rmmate wanted to share sngl rm w/famous artist. minimalist decor, compl furnished. FREE MEALS in intimate environmnt, avail immed. CALL anytime: 555–4915. Egon Schiele.

9. For Rent—COZY BACHELOR APT. priv entr., beautiful wdwrk, custm inter decor. CALL RIP–0000 MORTY B. GRAVES CO.

10. Roommate wanted—quiet singl prof'l seeks roommate to share upr East Side apt. WRKS NITES. Call during day fr appt. 555–6969.

11. Ultra lux. full studio. 500 sq. ft. renov. w/spectacular RIVR.VU backdrop. excel. fr students, artists. CALL MAGRITTE REALITY.

11. Thomas Sciacca

SOLUTION:

12. HEAVNLY pnthse apt for rent. airy, spacious w/ PANORAMIC VUS, extrmly hi ceiling, prtly furn. CALL 555–7682.

13. Rmmate wntd to share apt w/wllpar/fshion designer. Applicant MUST HVE OPN MIND. CALL 555–5293.

14. Roommate wanted—share apt in lux bldg, Cntrl Pk West. partly furn w/victorian antiq. MUST LIKE UNUSL PETS. CALL 555–7741.

15. Sunny 1 BR apt w/skylite, nr all trans. HEAT AND ELECTRIC NOT INCL. CALL 555–2367.

16. Roommate wanted/FEMALE PREF. to share lrge clean rm. lots of privacy as present occupant visits nbrs freq. CALL Norman: 555–8775

17. Space avail LRGE/OPN/FURN RM. pets allwd, great vu of park. dirt cheap. inquire: 555–2659. NO FEE.

18. Sngl mature wman wnts to share apt w/pet lover w/ no allergies. NO DOGS ALLWD, modest meals provd'd daily fr entire hsehld. Call before 5 P.M. 555–3838.

13. Anastasia Anderson

12. Xavier Wasowski

14. Barbara Reid

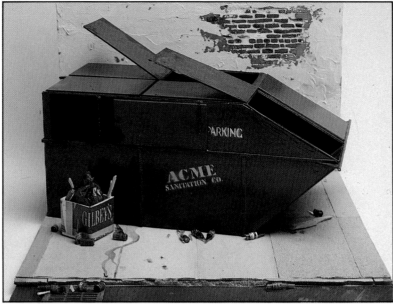

15. Bill Sponn

17. Rob Perota

16. Mickey Paraskevas

18. Michael Pinkus

SOLUTION:

20. Rainey Day King

19. Apartment to share— limited space still avail in 60's East studio. PREF QUIET MATURE ADULT. Call 555–8462

20. To Share—BIG 1 Bedrm APT. $795 MO. Call 555–0600.

21. Prof'l wanted to time-share brnstn office of PSY-CHOTHERPST. appropriatly furn, tasteful decor, West Village avail Tues/Wed/Thur ea wk. CALL 212–555–3673.

22. The Tombs 100 Centre Street offers 200 1-bdrm renov studios for rent. hi ceilings, a/c, all utilities, law library, conv wlk to dwntwn financial dist. avail immed. call KOCH AND ASSOCI-ATES, Realtors 555–1111.

23. Apartment for Rent— Newly renov and prtly furn. sofa bd w/w crpt. plenty of windows, LOCAT'N OPTN'L. $600 frst mo, $380 ea addt'l mo. CALL 555–8642.

24. Clean RECENTLY VA-CATED room. ELECTRIFY-ING decor, must see. CALL MORTROW REALTY 555–3210.

25. Apartment for Rent— custom renov by ownr. unusl bthrm w/imported tile flr clean, new appliances. LUXURY BLDG. 555–2000.

19. Dave Cutler

21. Dave Ridley

22. Elise Huber

24. Lorenzo Cardi

23. David Lusardi

25. Renee Russo

PROBLEM: APARTMENTS FOR RENT:
PROMOTION

Using type creatively, design a typographic image,
to be combined with art, for various promotional
pieces that express the concept of "Apartments for
Rent."

SPECIFICATIONS: INVITATION

Size: 5¼ by 7¼ inches.
Color: Four-color process.
Stock: Gloss-coated cover weight.
Printing: Offset lithography.

SPECIFICATIONS: POSTER 1

Size: 17 by 21 inches.
Color: Two colors
Stock: Gloss-coated text.
Printing: Offset lithography.

SPECIFICATIONS: POSTER 2

Size: 20 by 20 inches.
Color: Four-color process.
Stock: Gloss-coated text.
Printing: Offset lithography.

Darryl Ligasan

Invitation

Richard Sierra

Poster 1

Kam Mak

PROBLEM: EXTINCTION: THE BALD EAGLE   **SOLUTION:**

The bald eagle is a traditional American symbol. Unfortunately, this majestic bird is nearly extinct. The population of bald eagles had decreased radically for the following reasons:

- The elimination of breeding grounds caused by residential and industrial development.
- The ingestion of the pesticide DDT into their systems, which causes their eggs to hatch prematurely.
- Air pollution.
- Faulty high-tension wires.
- Hunters.

To instill a greater awareness of this situation, as a public service endeavor, convey this tragedy by creating an image that symbolizes the plight of the bald eagle.

SPECIFICATIONS

Size: 18 by 24 inches maximum.
Three-dimensional solutions:
18 by 18 by 18 inches maximum.
Color: Full color or black and white.
Medium: No limitation.

PROBLEM: EXTINCTION: PROMOTION

Employ various media to create a public service campaign to make people aware of the plight of the bald eagle.

SPECIFICATIONS: POSTER

Size: 23 by 33 inches.
Color: Four-color process.
Stock: Gloss-coated text.
Printing: Offset lithography.

SPECIFICATIONS: BUTTON

Size: 2½ by 2½ inches.
Color: Four-color process.
Printing: Offset lithography.

SPECIFICATIONS: ADVERTISEMENT

Size: 8½ by 11 inches.
Color: Four-color process.
Media: Consumer and trade magazines.

Robert Ehlers

Moses Kahn

Hiroko Tsuchihashi

Michael Donato

Extinction: The future state of the Bald Eagle? Being destroyed by pollution, pesticides, elimination of breeding areas and hunters. The School of Visual Arts and The Master Eagle Family of Companies present, The Bald Eagle: Survival or Extinction? On exhibit at The Master Eagle Gallery, 40 West 25th Street, 6th Floor. March 26th through May 4th, 1973. From 10 a.m. to 4 p.m. Monday through Friday.

Joseph Ianelli (Poster)

Louis Diaz (Button)

Louis Diaz (Advertisement)

181

PROBLEM: STAINED-GLASS CEILING   **SOLUTION:**

Design and execute a stained-glass ceiling to com-
memorate the bald eagle.

SPECIFICATIONS

Size: Ceiling: 12 by 35 feet.
Section size: 2½ by 5 feet.
Panel size (border): 15 by 18 inches.

Note: Over sixty students were selected to work on
this complex project. The major section that encompasses the entire bald eagle was a collaborative effort by the students. To ensure individual creative
input, each student designed a section of the
border.

Students of the School of Visual Arts

182

PROBLEM: SPORTS: THE TWENTY-FIRST CENTURY

SOLUTION:

By the twenty-first century, many sports may have changed radically in terms of rules, training techniques, equipment, stadiums, uniforms, broadcasting technology, and even the kind of men and women who will be participating. How do you think sports will change in the twenty-first century? This question was posed to outstanding sports personalities throughout the United States.

Choose one of the replies and interpret it. Your solution should capture the essence of the quotation you choose.

SPECIFICATIONS

Size: 18 by 24 inches maximum.
Three-dimensional solutions:
18 by 18 by 18 maximum.
Color: Full color or black and white.
Medium: No limitation.

"There will be more steps to lessen the pitcher's ability to strike the batters out. Maybe three balls, instead of four, making the plate smaller, lengthening the distance from the mound to home plate."

NOLAN RYAN
Baseball

"The competition will become even more fierce as our American games spread to other countries."

MERLIN OLSEN
Football

"I don't think we're headed for a *Rollerball* future. If we are, I'm glad O.J. will be retired."

O.J. SIMPSON
Football

Chuck Albano

Rick Zak

Tony Fiyalko

Choose a dramatic visual illustrating one of the statements about sports in the twenty-first century. Create a poster that includes this visual, the corresponding quotation, and the names of all the sports personalities who submitted predictions.

SPECIFICATIONS
Size: 23 by 27 inches.
Color: Four-color process.
Stock: Gloss-coated text.
Copy: Include quote illustrated and names of sports personalities who submitted predictions.
Printing: Offset lithography.

"Present unforms and protective equipment designs combine to make players seem awesomely bulky and squat. Uniforms of the future will have built-in body-contoured protection, and design will emphasize bright, sharp colors for an overall image of leanness and speed."

ROD GILBERT
Hockey

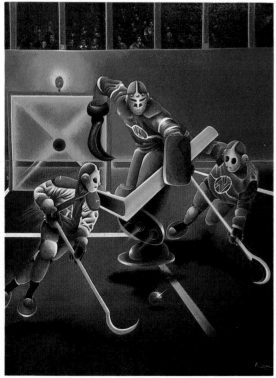

Kevin Unick

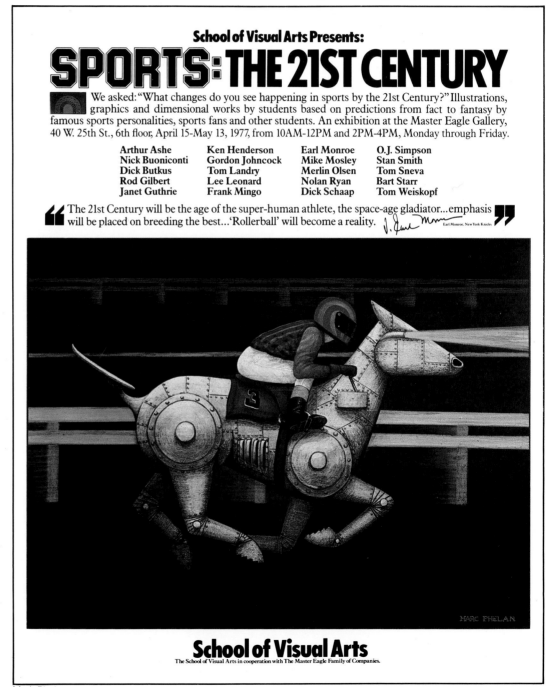

Mark Phelan

PROBLEM: DOUBLE TAKE

SOLUTION:

Investigate the idea of a double take as an exercise in understanding perception. People frequently react to familiar images in a conditioned way, seeing what they think they should see, rather than what is really there. A double take occurs when viewers realize their conditioned response is incorrect, that what they expected to see and thought they saw is not what actually exists.

Create, alter, or reinterpret an image in a way that makes people look twice.

SPECIFICATIONS

Size: 18 by 24 inches maximum.
Three-dimensional solutions:
18 by 18 by 18 inches maximum.
Color: Full color or black and white.
Medium: No limitation.

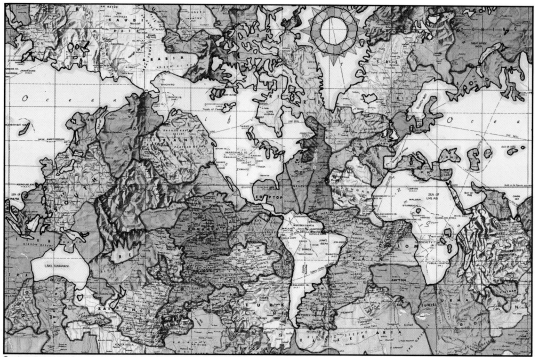
Carlos Alden

Kevin Unick

186

PROBLEM: DOUBLE TAKE: POSTER

SOLUTION:

Alter a well-known image to create a poster for an exhibition of double-take images.

SPECIFICATIONS

Size: 21 by 30 inches.
Color: Four-color process.
Stock: Gloss-coated text.
Printing: Offset lithography.

Judi Mintzer

PROBLEM: VISUAL PASSAGES

SOLUTION:

An ordinary map shows us how to get from one place to another. A visual map represents the transition from one event or condition to another. Visualize a sequence that occurs in the transition from one condition to another. Using a minimum of three and a maximum of twenty-five separate panels, convey the sequential transition. The ideas you can explore as subject matter for your visual passage are unlimited. The following are some examples:

- fat to thin
- love to hate
- sane to insane
- blue to green
- male to female
- civilian to soldier
- gourmet meal to a T.V. dinner

The ideas given above are examples only intended to increase your understanding of the problem. Draw freely on your own personal experience to create your visual passage.

SPECIFICATIONS

Size: 5 by 7 inches maximum.
Color: Full color or black and white.
Medium: No limitation.
Suggestions: Panels may be in one or a mixture of styles.

Gary Mele

Philip A. Morimitsu

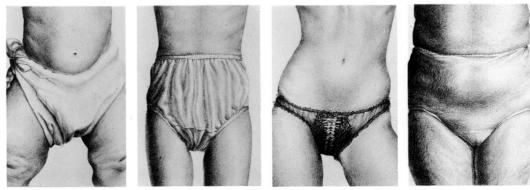

Cheryl Robin Levy

188

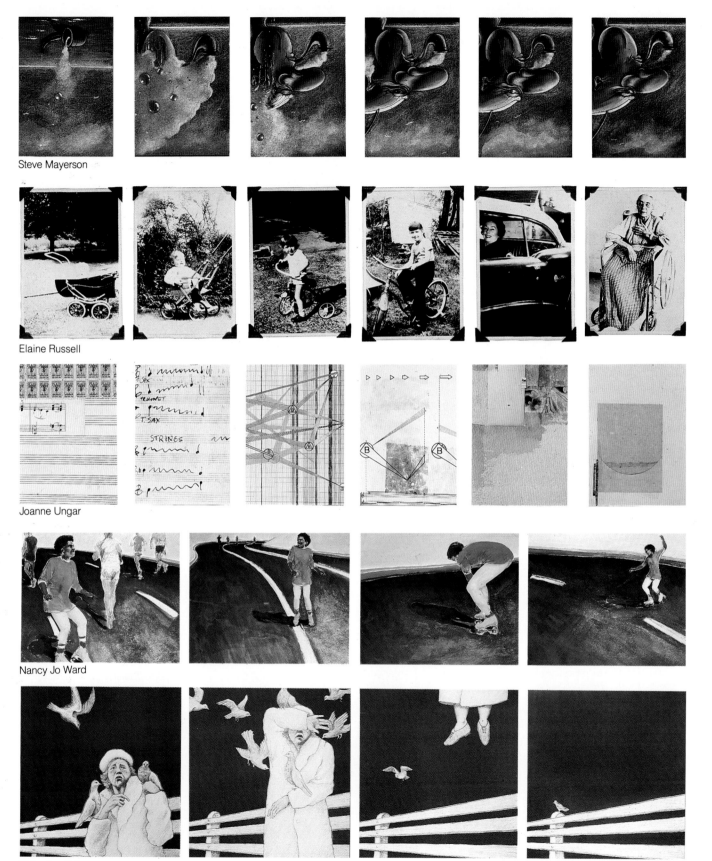

Steve Mayerson

Elaine Russell

Joanne Ungar

Nancy Jo Ward

Katherine Potter

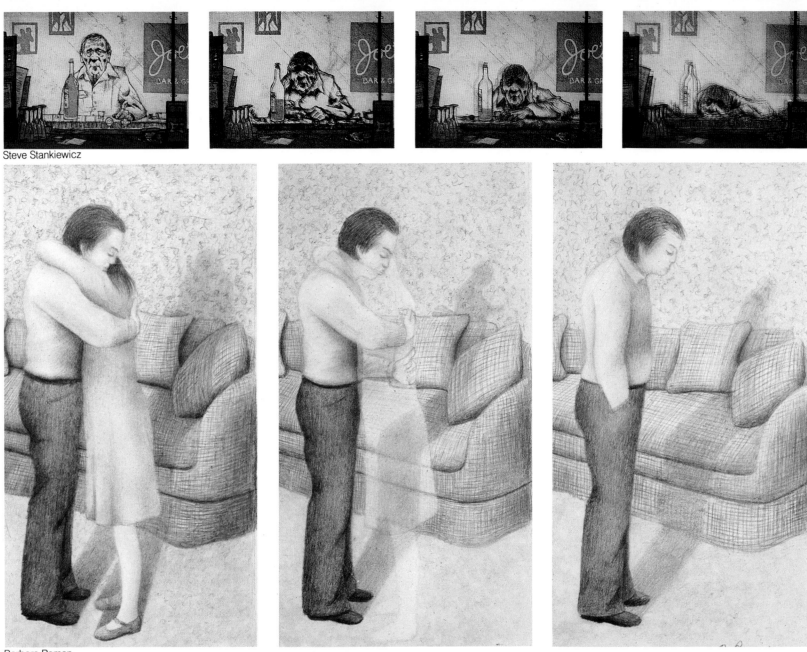

Steve Stankiewicz

Barbara Roman

Dave Galgano

SOLUTION:

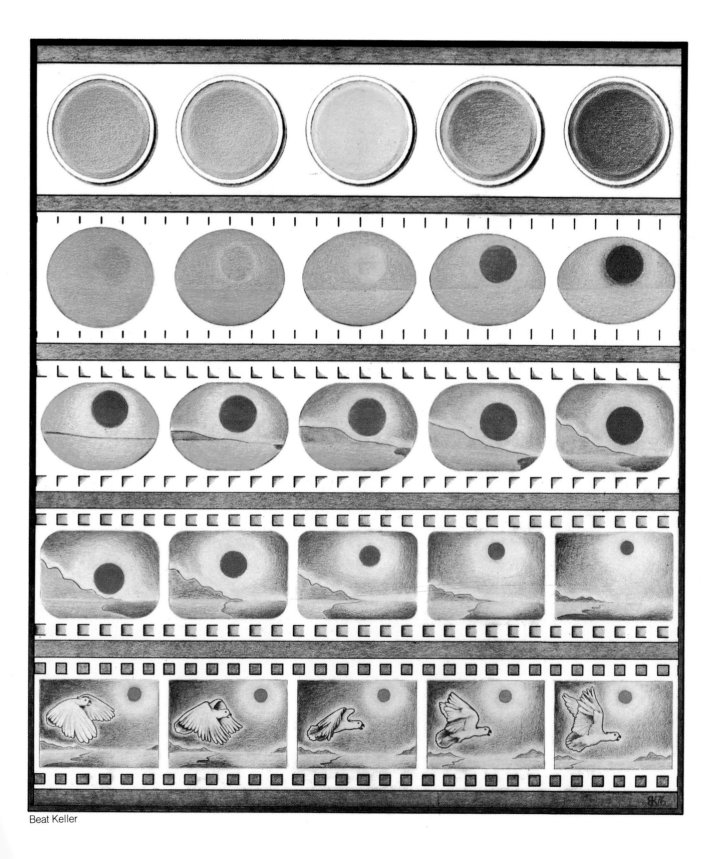

Beat Keller

Carmen Zeif

Chuck Albano

Design an invitation to an exhibition that best expresses the visual concept of sequential transition.

SPECIFICATIONS

Size: 5 by 7 inches.
Color: Full-color process.
Stock: Gloss-coated cover weight.
Printing: Offset lithography.

Nancy A. Viglietta

PROBLEM: AN ILLUSTRATION IS WORTH A
THOUSAND WORDS

The relationship of the illustrator to the writer is a
curious one. Most illustrators have to depict words
already written, over which they have no control.
This assignment reverses this process. You are to
create an illustration that expresses your views or
feelings on any given subject, and an author will
then interpret your illustration in words.

To implement this project, the following letter will be
sent to writers, inviting them to participate in this
assignment:

Dear Author:
A picture is worth a thousand words. I would like to
suggest that this old saying should also mean an
illustration is worthy of words! For an illustrator, the
artistic output of a whole career is based on the
words (stories, articles, poetry) of others. To provide
students with the rare opportunity to explore the
illustrator/writer relationship in reverse, a project
was organized around the premise that illustrations,
given to professional writers, can have words
created for them—one word, a sentence, or a whole
story. I hope you will decide to write something.
Enclosed you will find a slide of an illustration done
by a student and a page for your thoughts about it.

SPECIFICATIONS

Size: 18 by 24 inches maximum.
Three-dimensional solutions:
18 by 18 by 18 inches maximum.
Color: Full color or black and white.
Materials: No limitations.
Authors: The following is a partial listing of some of
the writers who will participate in this experimental
project:

Vance Bourjaily	Gael Greene
Kay Boyle	John Irving
Ray Bradbury	David Madden
Erskine Caldwell	Ron Padgett
Avery Corman	Irwin Shaw
Robert Creeley	Raymond Sokolov
Roald Dahl	Patti Stren
Lois Gould	R. B. Weber
Dan Greenberg	

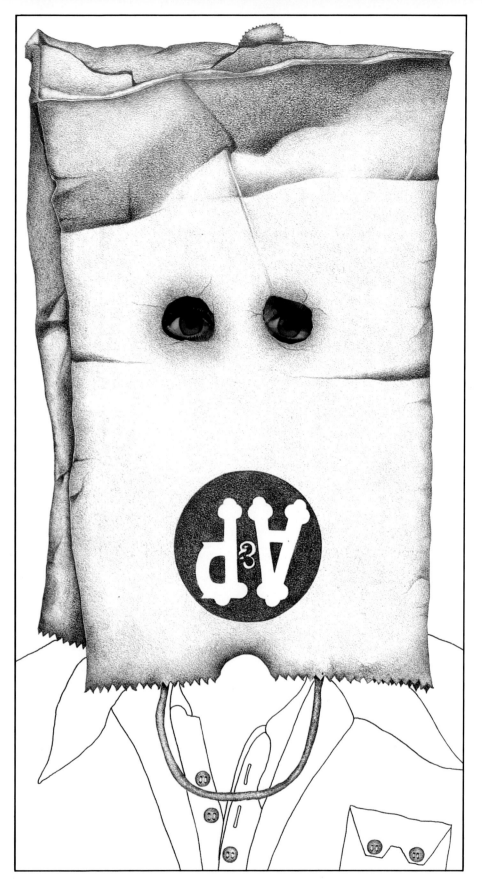

Illustrator: Patty Davidson

Writer: Ron Padgett; Poetry: *Triangles in the After-noon* (Sun, 1979); translation: *The Poet Assassi-nated by Guillaume Apollinaire* (North Point, 1984).

A picture is worth a thousand words is an old Chinese saying, isn't it?

Many Chinese words are, of course, pictures of what they represent. For example, the Chinese character for man resembles a stick figure of a man. Sort of. What is the Chinese character for "1,000" or for "word"?

It is true, nonetheless, that a picture is worth a thousand words. But no word can be equaled by a picture of what the word represents. So words and pictures are interrelated but not interchangeable. (Try to draw a picture of that sentence.) Words and pictures are almost united in the art of sign language, in which the fingers make quick sketches in the air. Or in the Walker Evans photograph of the gigantic word DAMAGED being loaded onto a truck.

Sound movies are more various than silent ones and therefore give the impression of being more real. Good painting is more various than bad painting; the latter always looks the same. The former often looks different. Cézanne's good paintings have a way of being different each time one sees them. I wave a museum guard over to one of them, a watercolor of Mont Ste.-Victoire. I point to it. This means I am very hungry for lunch. Which way to the lunchroom please?

. . . worth a thousand words." I feel certain that we are not expected to take this literally, i.e., 1 picture = 1,000 words. The expression "a thousand" probably means "very many," as in "a thousand pardons, O great Omar," and not as in "a thousand dollars, O great Omar."

(In some primitive cultures—I do not remember which—the number one stands for a single thing, the number two stands for two of these things, but the number three means simply "many.")

"A picture is worth a thousand words" consists of seven words, or approximately .1429 of a picture. But .1429 of a picture cannot express what these seven words do. A thousand pictures cannot.

"Words! Pictures!" Yak yak. You think you're so smart. "Pictures!" Yak yak. "Words!" You make me sick. Why don't you take a walk with a sack over your head. And stay there for several hundred years.

The shock of her presence in the room is intense, as if her skin were giving off quantities of light. Everything else looks dull by comparison: the rectangle of the bed, with mashed and twisted pillows and the striped spread, the little rug, the curtains, walls, table, paint table, easel: all but the eyes of the painter, which are blazing, as if feeding on the energy radiated by the model.

His eyes dart from model to canvas, canvas to model. They know nothing in between. The lifelessness of the surroundings; the air in the room; the events of the previous night; his own body; his legs in their stockings, his body sheathed in clothing, covered with a spattered and stained smock; the very hand that obeys the directives activated by the model's energy: he seems utterly unaware of all these, as he seems equally unaware of the approaching evening, the approaching years, the approaching grave, the approaching degeneration of the sun, the complete extinction of human consciousness, tinged with the hope of divine rescue. It is as if the spirit of the painter had been drawn out of his body and stretched along his line of sight, from model to canvas, canvas to model, brilliant as sunbeams through leaves on a suddenly bright afternoon.

He seems unaware, even, of the, yes, the possibility of swelling, at first a suggestion of an autonomous growing, a mounting bulge, a foreign presence which suddenly floods his groin with a triumphant rush of sensation, and his penis strains against the cloth, a lost Atlantis arisen in his pants.

And then it does seem for a moment as though he might be dimly aware of it, as the model rises and stretches her limbs and strolls over to the canvas, for he glances down at the front of his frock and sees streaks of burnt umber, rose madder, violet, and ultramarine mashed into sudden bristling daubs of white and twists of yellow and tan over red and blue streaks. The model gazes at her likeness for a while, tilts her head, and steps back. The artist steps forward to correct the arm, and as he does so, the mound is visible beneath the frock. The model gives a little jump, and the artist's eyes glaze over with a small wave of fright.

SOLUTION:

Illustrator: Joseph Bonanni

Writer: David Madden; Writer in Residence at Louisiana State University since 1968. Native of Knoxville, Tennessee. Author of nine works of fiction, including *Cassandra Singing, Bijou, The Suicide's Wife, The Shadow Knows, The New Orleans of Possibilities,* and of twenty works of nonfiction, including *Harlequin's Stick, Charlie's Cane, Cain's Craft, The Poetic Image in Six Genres, Rediscoveries, Remembering James Agee, Tough Guy Writers of the Thirties.*

The Jealous Mouth

Unable to experience his own existence physically, a genius, whose potential had gone unrealized for half a century, filled his house with mirrors. He never stood and stared into them, but always gazed at them in passing.

One day, as he passed the mirrors, actual bodies stepped out of them, each with an erection, each a moron.

The morons accompanied him everywhere he went, until finally he had to be shut away. His desperate efforts to find mirrors were too often successful, creating the problem of warehousing the morons he propagated.

In the belief that only following his death would his legion of morons languish and die, a guard, encouraged by others, set the genius up, and fellow inmates killed him.

But his 3,507 images did not languish and die. They are housed in separate asylums throughout the world, under heavy sedation, unable to reproduce, even in the presence of mirrors.

But one of them whispers in gibberish that when it turns its back on the mirror and sits in the corner of its room, it feels cool air beating on the back of its neck, sees shadows floating on the floor, hears nothing, and it moans that somewhere someone is painting a picture of the room, leaving it out.

The World's One Breathing

For the world's one breathing . . .
   a sales representative, startled from a deep doze by a voice saying crisply, "It's not the end of the world," sees nothing from the jetliner window one moment, squints at sunlight the next.
   a woman wearing an apron slides the glass doors open with one hand, holding a cup of steaming black coffee in the other, about to step into bird song in her patio, stops, seeing a bird lying on the flag-stone, quivering
         in his sideview mirror, a nervous young man, driving alone, watches the erratic movements of the U-haul trailer he is pulling, thinks for a moment he has lost it, then watches it swing back into view
         as his father holds a mirror up to his grandmother's mouth, shaking his head, a boy imagines the beating of wings

         the front, side, and rear windows of a junked bus mirror 365,389 passengers and 1,250,000 miles of Guatemala
         his back to the mirror, a writer, sitting at his desk, sneezes violently, convulsively, three times, spraying page 483
         on Avery Island, a car backfires, startling 207 white cranes into flight
         in a clear mountain stream, a bear shatters its image
                     . . . may at first attain true time

The Triumph of Common Sense

First of all, cranes positively do not fly out of mirrors. To back up my thesis, I have consulted *The American Heritage Dictionary of the English Language,* which does not lie or mislead, as poetry and art do. First, I looked up "mirror," to determine whether mirrors have, even in the remotest way, any properties that would allow cranes (I assume no claim has been made that birds other than cranes can perform the feat) to enter through the silver backs of and proceed to fly out the glass fronts of mirrors. Allow me to quote: "Any surface capable of reflecting sufficient undiffused light to form a virtual image of an object placed in front of it." The key words are "reflecting" and *"in front of."* Second, I turned to "crane." And again I quote: "Any of various large wading birds of the family Gruidae, having a long neck, long legs, and a long bill." The term "crane" may also be applied "loosely" to similar birds, such as the heron. And, of course, we are all familiar with another use of the word "crane," as, quote, "a machine for hoisting and moving heavy objects by means of cables attached to a movable boom." No matter how hard you "crane," i.e., "strain and stretch (the neck) . . . for a better view" (I am quoting), it is as easy for a machine-crane as it is for a bird-crane to pass through a mirror, as defined above, without breaking it to smithereens. As in meaning 2.a. in my dictionary ("to balk and lean forward, as a horse before jumping") and 2.b. ("to hesitate"), the person of common sense must conclude with me that what the picture depicts is preposterous. If it were not, we might reasonably expect the dictionary to posit the possibility. Even Shakespeare spoke of "holding a mirror up to nature." He is not known to have imagined a creature of nature invading the silver backing of a mirror and flying out the front. Cranes do not fly through mirrors. I repeat. Cranes do not fly through mirrors. I repeat. Cranes do not fly through mirrors. I repeat.

SOLUTION:

Illustrator: Peter Vey

Writer: Robert Creeley; Poetry: *Memory Gardens*
(New Directions, 1986); *Collected Poems, 1945–
1975* (University of California Press, 1983); *Mirrors*
(New Directions, 1983).

Blue Moon

The chair's still there,
but the goddamn sun's
gone red again—

and instead of Mabel
there is a potato,
or something like that there,

sitting like it owned the place.
It's got no face
and it won't speak to anyone.

I'm scared.
If I had legs
I'd run.

Illustrator: Karen Pietrobono

Writer: Patti Stren; Children's books: *Hug Me* (Harper and Row, 1977); *Bo the Constrictor* (Greentree Publishers, Canada, 1978); *Sloan and Philamina* (Dutton [Unicorn Books], 1978); *I Never Met a Monster I Didn't Like,* coloring book (Flying Rabbit, 1975); Annual Report: *The Pennsylvania Public Television Network Commission* (1977).

I see this drawing as part of a series of illustrations for a story all about an elephant . . "A SADIE" WHO WANTS TO BE A DANCER.

I picture Sadie this way. She's unlike other elephants who are happy doing all the normal things that elephants do . . . like eating peanuts, taking long, quiet strolls and just standing around looking gray and doing nothing. This Sadie is not content, she wants more out of life! She wants to be a dancer! Here's the idea for the story . . .

Sadie didn't think being big had anything to do with being a dancer. "You're either a dancer or you're not," she said. "It's a feeling inside you and I have that feeling."

The other elephants thought she should take life easy but Sadie didn't. She had to dance. She'd pirouette around telephone poles, leap across the dining room and boogie while baking brownies.

Sadie then joined Miss Gladys' dance class where, after finally squeezing into an extra large size 35 leotard, she practiced being graceful to "Every Little Breeze Seems to Whisper Louise" and earned the lead role in the class recital. It was the first time ever that an elephant was the swan princess. And, as Sadie leaped and threw herself into the air with the beauty and grace of a true ballerina, she knew at last that she was a dancer.

Illustrator: Robert Lieber

Writer: Vance Bourjaily; Novel: *Brill among the Ruins* (Dial Press, 1971).

Robin and I got into a father-daughter argument about the contents of the sky. She said stars, I said gulls. She said stars, I said butterflies. She said stars, I said potato chips. She said she has younger eyes. Robin, being twelve, is quite right. It was cold and wet outside; we like the illustration, and wished we were there.
    Robin Bourjaily, mostly.

Umbrella smiles and sunburn styles
Short sleeve cars ride by.
August notes September coats.
As the stars fall from the sky.
    Robert Lieber

SOLUTIONS:

Illustrator: Janet Brignolia

Writer: R. B. Weber; Poetry: *The Fishing-Print Poems* (Street Press, 1984); *Poems from the Xenia Hotel* (Street Press, 1979); *Laurie's Songs* (Street Press, 1976, 1978). Poems have appeared in a number of periodicals, including *Broadside, Confrontation, Bluefish, Zephyr,* and *Xanadu.* Teaches creative writing, literature, and film appreciation at Southamptom College of Long Island University.

romance waits, waits. and waits . . .

There in front of splashes of burnt
sienna chair a huge cupid-
bow of lips parts lascivious
smears of promises. A blue
awning of hat shades sunken,
hidden eyes. A head shadows
itself against a mirror. All
the face strives but twists aside.
One golden touch of earring dangles
the only surprise. A flat white
column of neck and chest slides
down within a blue cloth frame.
Where do volcanic hearts
of expectation beat us to?

Using one of the illustrations that was written about,
design a poster that expresses the concept An Illustration Is Worth A Thousand Words.

SPECIFICATIONS

Size: 22 by 37 inches.
Color: Four-color process.
Stock: Gloss-coated text.
Copy: Include author's written material.
Printing: Offset lithography.

Moving from the hypothetical to the real is a major step in one's education. The following projects were all real jobs, not teacher-created assignments, rare but welcome opportunities at the college level. Accepting jobs and entrusting their solutions to students requires a unique situation in which students, faculty, administrators, and clients work together, each being aware of all criteria to be met. Most of these projects were team efforts in which students acted as art director, designer, illustrator, or photographer.

PROBLEM: PROMOTIONAL POSTER

SOLUTION:

Using the bicentennial of the United States of America as a theme, design a poster promoting a typesetter's establishment. Include a wide range of their display typefaces. The poster should be soft-sell in nature, implying the creative leadership of the client in the industry. Keep in mind that the client is also a photoengraver; the solution should show the client's expertise in this area as well.

SPECIFICATIONS

Size: 24 by 36 inches.
Color: Four-color process.
Stock: Gloss-coated text.
Printing: Offset lithography.
Requirement: The logo of the Master Eagle Family of Companies must appear prominently in the poster.
Client: The Master Eagle Family of Companies, New York.

PROBLEM: METRIC POSTER

All of the major countries in the world except the United States use metric units of measure. Many people feel the United States should adopt this system as well. Design a poster that will help the American public adapt to metrics.

Commercial clients often promote public service issues as a means of self-promotion. While educating the public, they are raising awareness of their company as well.

SPECIFICATIONS

Size: 24 by 36 inches.
Color: Four-color process.
Stock: Gloss-coated text.
Printing: Offset lithography.
Requirement: The logo of the Master Eagle Family of Companies must appear prominently in the poster.
Client: The Master Eagle Family of Companies, New York.

Jo-Ann Rosiello

SOLUTION:

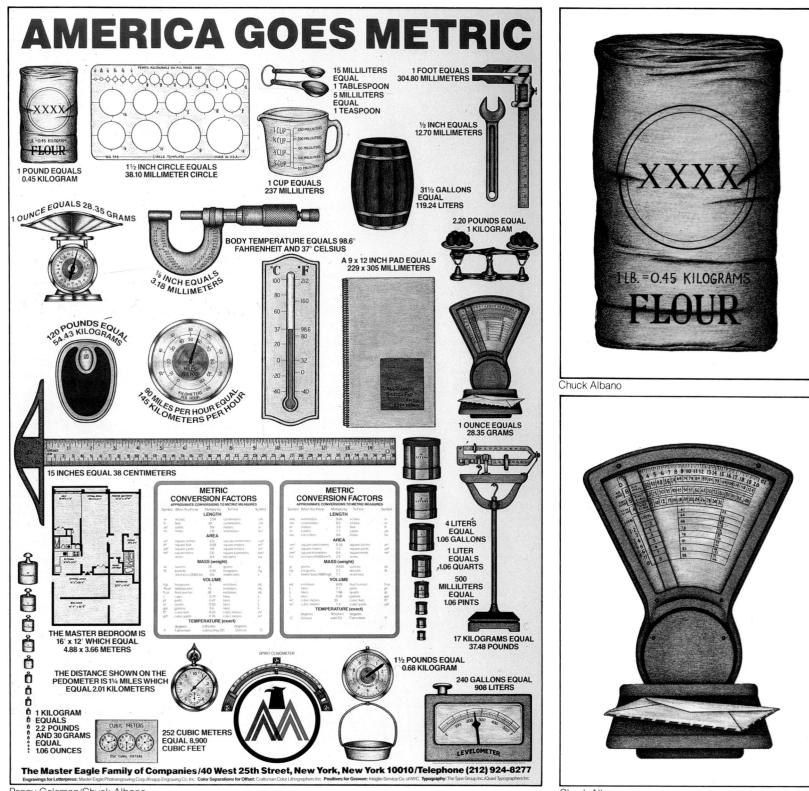

Penny Coleman/Chuck Albano

Chuck Albano

Chuck Albano

PROBLEM: OLYMPIC CACHET

SOLUTION:

Design the cachet collection for the 1980 Olympic Games held at Lake Placid, New York. The topics include all the events and ceremonies that took place during the competition. Choose at least one of the following topics:

Olympic Torch Flight
Opening Ceremonies of the 1980 Winter Olympic Games
Opening of the Olympic Village at Ray Brook
Opening Ceremonies for the National Fine Arts Program
Opening of the 82nd IOC Session
Ecumenical Religious Service
Pairs Freeskating Competition
1,000-meter Men's Speed-Skating Race
1980 Winter Olympic Games Hockey Competition
3,000-meter Women's Speed-Skating Event
Women's Giant Slalom
10-kilometer Women's Cross-Country Race
90-meter Ski Jump Competition
4 x 7.5-kilometer Biathalon Relay
Men's Downhill Race
Two-Man Bobsled Race
Finals of the Men's and Women's Luge Competition
Closing Ceremony of the 1980 Winter Olympic Games

The key to this assignment is identifying the essence of each event or ceremony and then designing for it accordingly. Since the small size of the image is a limitation, a symbolic application may be needed to communicate the intended message. Consider Ludwig Mies van der Rohe's dictum "Less Is More" when solving this problem.

SPECIFICATIONS

Size: Envelope: 3⅝ by 6½ inches.
Image: 2 by 3 inches.
Color: Choose two of the following official Olympic colors: PMS-299, blue; PMS-109, yellow; PMS-361, green; PMS-warm red; PMS-reflex blue; PMS-black; PMS-430, gray (60%).
Stock: 100% rag content envelope.
Printing: Steel engraving.
Copy: Use copy as given for each specific cachet.
Typography: Choose one of the official Olympic typefaces: Optima; Optima Medium; Optima Bold; Korinna; Korinna Medium; Korinna Bold; Helvetica; Helvetica Medium.
Requirement: The Lake Placid Olympic logo will be no larger than ½ by ⅝ inch and will be placed without letters but with the Olympic rings. It can be positioned in the cachet design as the artist sees fit.

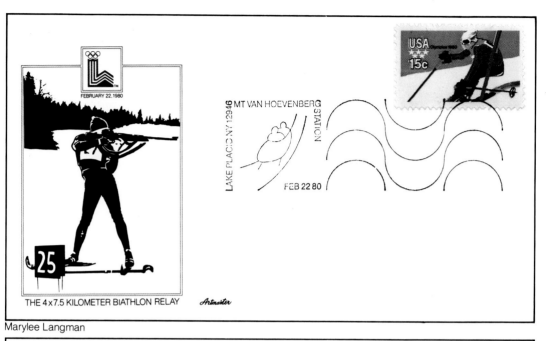

Marylee Langman

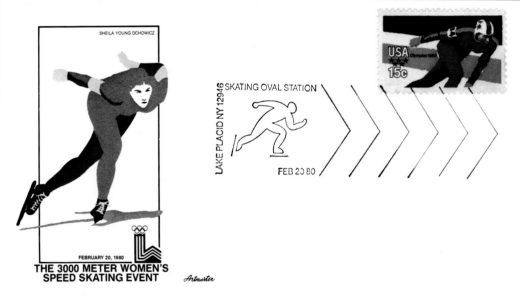

Susan Huber

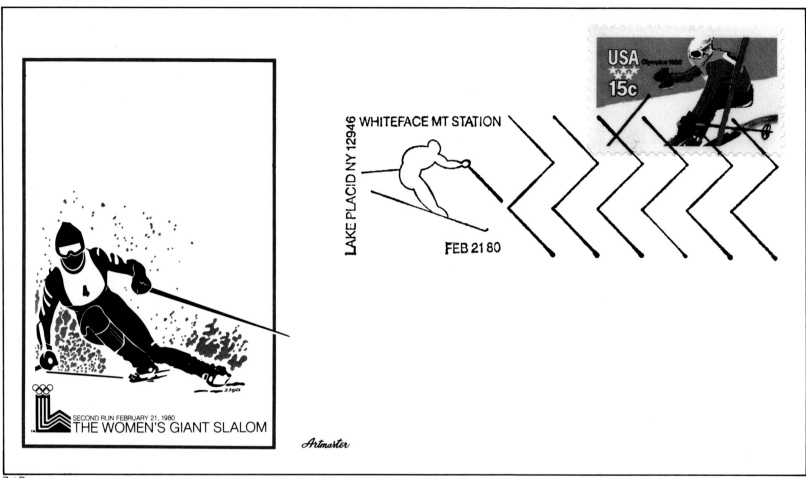

Zvi Rosen

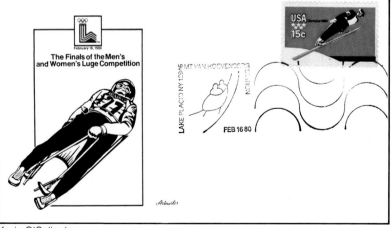

Rush Hinsdale

Kevin O'Callaghan

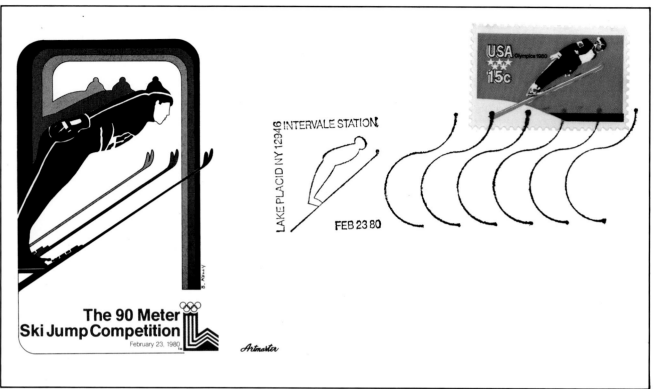

Brian Kelly

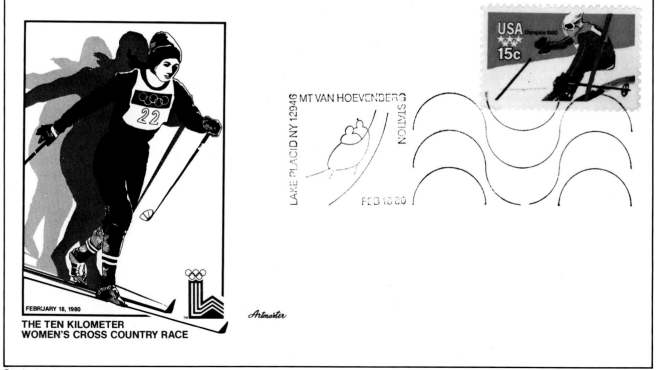

Corrin Jacobsen

FEBRUARY 14,1980

THE MEN'S DOWNHILL RACE

Zvi Rosen

Zvi Rosen

Mary Van Bodegan

David Bayer

Ayelet Bender

PROBLEM: PUBLIC ADVERTISING SYSTEM
To create an alternative to what many students felt was an overly materialistic orientation toward advertising.

SOLUTION:

If you need advertising and can't afford it, call us up.

If you have an organization with a cause: if you represent a movement, a human rights group, a consumer group, you can probably use our help.
We'll inform the public about you, help you to raise money and volunteers, by advertising your message.
And we'll do it for free.
We're a group of advertising professionals and students who can work with you to produce ads, posters, pamphlets, booklets, leaflets, commercials-even films.
Let us put our talent, enthusiasm and production resources to work for you.
We'll give you everything we've got.

PAS
Public Advertising System

555-7350 Ext. 29

The above advertisement marked the birth of a school advertising agency called the Public Advertising System (PAS). This organization gave students the opportunity to use their creative skills in designing ads for agencies and nonprofit groups. The students created the ads and oversaw them through the entire production process.

PROBLEM 1: To make women aware of the importance of self-examination for the detection of breast cancer and to encourage professional checkups when necessary.
CLIENT: American Cancer Society.

PROBLEM 2: To urge all black parents to have their children tested for sickle cell disease.
CLIENT: Foundation for Research and Education in Sickle Cell Disease.

Last week I found a lump in my breast.

"I was scared to death that it might be cancer but I was afraid to go to the doctor.
"After a couple of weeks I finally went. He made some tests and told me that it was a good thing that I hadn't waited any longer or I might have had to have my breast removed.
"I am having some treatments now and will be well again soon.
"Learn how to check yourself regularly and if you suspect __anything__ see your doctor."

Lie down. Put one hand behind your head. With the other hand, fingers flattened, gently feel your breast. Press ever so lightly.

This illustration shows you how to check each breast. Begin at the top and follow the arrows, feeling gently for a lump or thickening.

Now repeat the same procedure sitting up, with hand still behind your head.

The School of Visual Arts Public Advertising System

1

YOUR HEALTHY LOOKING CHILD MAY HAVE SICKLE CELL DISEASE.

You can be fooled.
Your child may look healthy but have a mild form of the disease called Sickle Cell Trait.
Some symptoms are blood in the urine and stomach pain.
The severe form of the disease is called Sickle Cell Anemia.
Some symptoms are easy fatigue, bed wetting, pain in legs and stomach.
The only sure way to know whether your child has the disease is to get a test.

WHERE TO GET TESTED:
Jamaica Hospital:
89th Avenue & Van Wyck Expressway, Jamaica, N.Y.
St. Luke's Hospital Center:
421 West 113th Street, New York, N.Y.
Sydenham Hospital:
Manhattan Avenue at 123rd Street, New York, N.Y.
Morrisania Hospital:
Out-Patient Clinic—Adults and Children
Walton Avenue & 168th Street, Bronx, N.Y.
Kings County Hospital:
Out-Patient Clinic—Adults-Pediatric
Pediatric Clinic—Children,
451 Clark Avenue, Brooklyn, N.Y.
For further information write:
Foundation for Research and Education in Sickle Cell Disease ©
423-431 West 120th Street,
New York, N.Y. 10027. Telephone: (212) 222-8500.

PAS
PUBLIC ADVERTISING SYSTEM
A DIVISION OF THE SCHOOL OF VISUAL ARTS SCHOLARSHIP FUND
PRINTED AT THE SCHOOL OF VISUAL ARTS BY THE VISUAL ARTS PRESS

2

PROBLEM 3: To make the public aware of the
problem of child abuse.
CLIENT: The Society for the Prevention of Cruelty to
Children.

"She beats me a lot. But I know she loves me 'cause she tells me that.
The neighbors say she's sick and needs help. I hope she'll get better. Then when
I go home we'll be happy and I won't be hurt anymore."

Joan's mother is a child abuser. Of course, she loves Joan. But she needs
expert counseling and attention. Friends recognized the problem, and the
Society for the Prevention of Cruelty to Children was made aware of the
situation. Now, both Joan and her mother are getting the attention they need.
Soon their family can be reunited. Give other families like Joan's a second
chance. If you know of a child being abused, your call will help.

442-5511
The Society for the Prevention of Cruelty to Children
School of Visual Arts Public Advertising System

PHOTO: KEN AMBROSE

3

SOLUTION:

PROBLEMS 4–7: To eliminate the stigma of having a venereal disease and to inform young adults of the various clinics for treatment.
CLIENT: New York City Health Department.

PROBLEM 8: To promote free prenatal care at a community health clinic.
CLIENT: Nena Health Center.

PROBLEM 9: To encourage children to join their neighborhood community center.
CLIENT: Grand Street Settlement House.

PROBLEM 10: To inform women of the dangers of improper prenatal care.
CLIENT: New York City Health Department

PROBLEM 11: To inform deaf people of a community center just for them.
CLIENT: Office of Continuing Education, District 11 (Community Center for the Deaf).

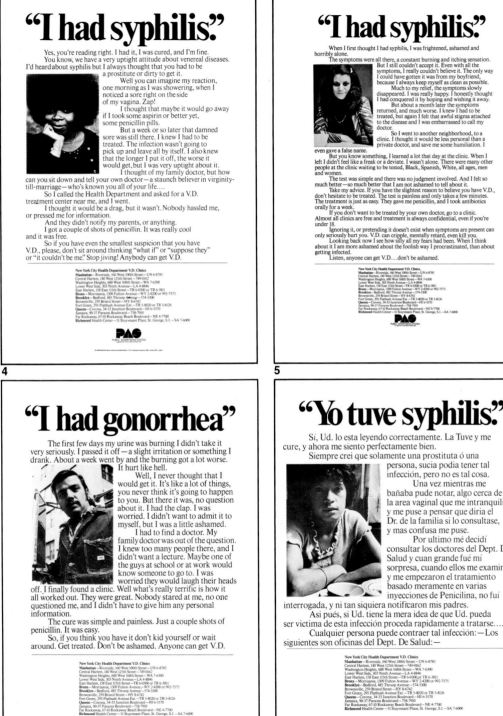

4

5

6

7

8

Love's not enough. You need pre-natal care.
When you're pregnant you need help and someone friendly to talk to, and we have it.
We have exercise classes, films, counseling and all the medical services that you need.
Come see us or give us a call. The Nena Health Center 290 East 3rd St. N.Y.C. Telephone 677-5040
The School of Visual Arts Public Advertising System

9

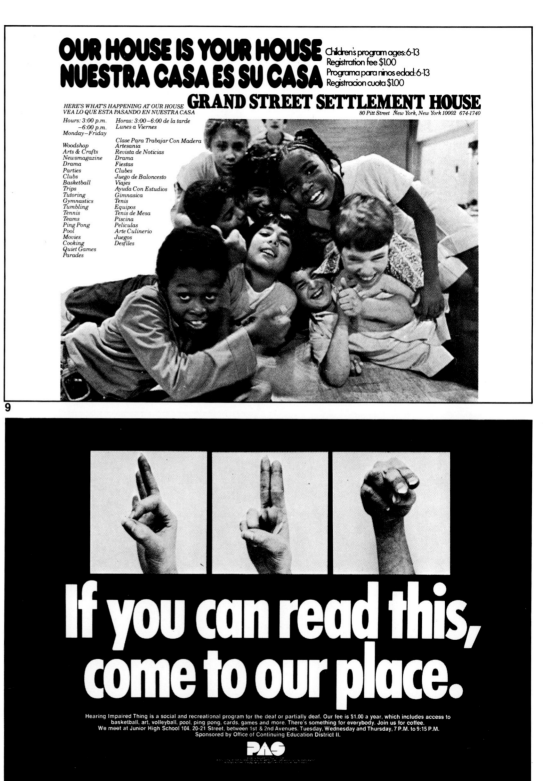

OUR HOUSE IS YOUR HOUSE
NUESTRA CASA ES SU CASA

Children's program ages: 6-13
Registration fee $1.00
Programa para ninos edad: 6-13
Registracion cuota $1.00

GRAND STREET SETTLEMENT HOUSE

HERE'S WHAT'S HAPPENING AT OUR HOUSE
VEA LO QUE ESTA PASANDO EN NUESTRA CASA

80 Pitt Street New York, New York 10002 674-1740

Hours: 3:00 p.m.   *Horas: 3:00–6:00 de la tarde*
*   –6:00 p.m.*   *Lunes a Viernes*
Monday–Friday

Woodshop	*Clase Para Trabajar Con Madera*
Arts & Crafts	*Artesania*
Newsmagazine	*Revista de Noticias*
Drama	*Drama*
Parties	*Fiestas*
Clubs	*Clubes*
Basketball	*Juego de Baloncesto*
Trips	*Viajes*
Tutoring	*Ayuda Con Estudios*
Gymnastics	*Gimnasica*
Tumbling	*Tenis*
Tennis	*Equipos*
Teams	*Tenis de Mesa*
Ping Pong	*Piscina*
Pool	*Peliculas*
Movies	*Arte Culinerio*
Cooking	*Juegos*
Quiet Games	*Desfiles*
Parades	

10

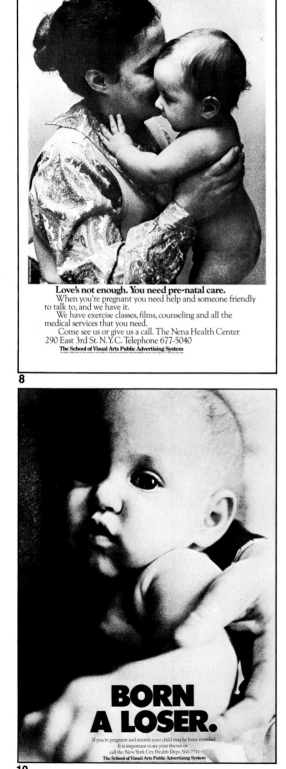

BORN
A LOSER.

If you're pregnant and anemic your child may be born retarded.
It is important to see your doctor or
call the New York City Health Dept. 566-7711
The School of Visual Arts Public Advertising System

11

If you can read this,
come to our place.

Hearing Impaired Thing is a social and recreational program for the deaf or partially deaf. Our fee is $1.00 a year, which includes access to basketball, art, volleyball, pool, ping pong, cards, games and more. There's something for everybody. Join us for coffee.
We meet at Junior High School 104, 20-21 Street, between 1st & 2nd Avenues, Tuesday, Wednesday and Thursday, 7 P.M. to 9:15 P.M.
Sponsored by Office of Continuing Education District II.

PAS

213

SOLUTION:

Create an advertising campaign that will raise public consciousness about and help dispel prejudice toward the disabled.
CLIENT: President's Commiittee on the Employment of the Handicapped.

PROBLEMS 12–15: To show the accomplishments of the disabled.
CLIENT: President's Committee on the Employment of the Handicapped.

PROBLEMS 16–18: To show that disabled people have the same feelings and needs that others do.
CLIENT: President's Committee on the Employment of the Handicapped.

PROBLEMS 19–21: To eliminate prejudice toward the retarded.
CLIENT: President's Committee on the Employment of the Handicapped.

Don Dreyer teaches a class in Public Relations at Hofstra University from a wheelchair.

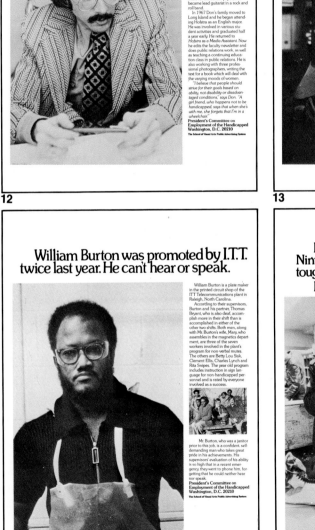

Don Dreyer has Osteogenesis Imperfecta—brittle bones. At age five he started falling. By the time his condition was diagnosed at age 14, he had had 20 breaks in his legs. He spent most of his childhood indoors, and was tutored at home. Because they had a special home room class for the handicapped, he was able to attend Sheepshead Bay High School in Brooklyn. The transition was, for him, like that of "a butterfly emerging from a cocoon." He earned high grades, joined various clubs, wrote for the school paper, and became lead guitarist in a rock and roll band.

In 1967 Don's family moved to Long Island and he began attending Hofstra as an English major. He was involved in various student activities and graduated half a year early. He returned to Hofstra as a *Media Assistant*. Now he edits the faculty newsletter and does public relations work, as well as teaching a continuing education class in public relations. He is also working with three professional photographers, writing the text for a book which will deal with the varying moods of women.

"I believe that people should strive for their goals based on ability, not disability or disadvantaged conditions," says Don. *"A girl friend, who happens not to be handicapped, says that when she's with me, she forgets that I'm in a wheelchair."*
President's Committee on Employment of the Handicapped Washington, D.C. 20210
The School of Visual Arts Public Advertising System

12

George V. Eltgroth is a Patent Attorney for General Electric. He is legally blind.

George Eltgroth's official title is Counsel for Patent Strategy and Utilization. His work for the International Division of GE involves finding people who infringe on GE patents and handling cross-licensing agreements between major corporations.

Eltgroth is 62. When he was 33, he contracted polio. It took him two years before he was able to walk with a cane. At 41 his vision dropped below the level of legal blindness. But, as Eltgroth points out, "There wasn't anyone who was going to look after me. I had four small children. I had to continue my career." In 1964, Eltgroth negotiated one quarter of GE's acquisition of Compagnie des Machines Bulle from Olivetti. He was put in charge of patent operations in Phoenix, Milan, and Paris. "I had 20 French lawyers working for me," says Eltgroth, "only two of whom spoke English. So I learned French, not from books, but by ear." Eltgroth is also fluent in German and is able to work in Spanish as well.

"Handling forms is hard for me," says Eltgroth. "I have only peripheral vision about 1 or 2 percent of normal. I read slowly, so I have to do a lot of preparatory work for patent negotiations. My handwriting is weak, so I type. I have physical problems, but by developing my abilities in law and technology, I'm able to make the balance come out positive. I've wrapped up negotiations that would have taken most non-handicapped people five years in two. When you're handicapped, you've got to test your limits. As a result of my polio, falling is dangerous—ice and snow are a problem. So I put screws in the bottom of my galoshes. When I had crutches, I put hooks on them for my briefcase. You shouldn't dwell on what's lost, but on what you have left."
President's Committee on Employment of the Handicapped Washington, D.C. 20210
The School of Visual Arts Public Advertising System

13

William Burton was promoted by I.T.T. twice last year. He can't hear or speak.

William Burton is a plate maker in the printed circuit shop of the ITT Telecommunications plant in Raleigh, North Carolina.

According to their supervisors, Burton and his partner, Thomas Bryant, who is also deaf, accomplish more in their shift than is accomplished in either of the other two shifts. Both men, along with Mr. Burton's wife, Mary, who assembles in the magnetics department, are three of the seven workers involved in the plant's program for non-verbal mutes. The others are Betty Lou Sisk, Clement Ellis, Charles Lynch and Rita Snipes. The year old program includes instruction in sign language for non-handicapped personnel and is rated by everyone involved as a success.

Mr. Burton, who was a janitor prior to this job, is a confident, self-demanding man who takes great pride in his achievements. His supervisors' evaluation of his ability is so high that in a recent emergency, they went to phone him, forgetting that he could neither hear nor speak.
President's Committee on Employment of the Handicapped Washington, D.C. 20210
The School of Visual Arts Public Advertising System

14

Lt. Edward Mamet is Commander of the Ninth Precinct Investigations Unit, one of the toughest police commands in N.Y.C. He has one leg.

"When I first came out of the hospital," says Edward Mamet, "people didn't know how to treat me. They had to act nice, open doors . . . it's awkward. Even this one ranking officer with a reputation for chewing people out kept treating me with kid gloves. I felt alot better when, after about two weeks, he saw I was getting around alright, and started treating me like everyone else . . ."

Lt. Edward Mamet was 37 when he lost his left leg in an accident three years ago. Everyone encouraged him to take his $14,000 pension and retire, but he refused. He had been on his way up, and he felt that if he retired he would just vegetate. He convinced his superiors to return him to duty, but out of concern for his safety they gave him a desk job. Paperwork was the last thing he wanted to do. With the help of the police surgeon, who declared him fit for active service, he was able to obtain a transfer. Soon after, he earned a promotion. Now he's supervising a team of 14 detectives and a sergeant, investigating unsolved crimes on the Lower East Side. He feels he does almost as well as before, and intends eventually to become a captain.

"I've chosen to perform," he says, "therefore I have to prove I can do it." He tests himself constantly. During New York's coldest and iciest winter in 90 years, he did not slip once.
President's Committee on Employment of the Handicapped Washington, D.C. 20210
The School of Visual Arts Public Advertising System

15

16

I do. I think. I feel.

The President's Committee on Employment of the Handicapped
The School of Visual Arts Public Advertising System

17

I do.
I think.
I feel.

The President's Committee on Employment of the Handicapped
The School of Visual Arts Public Advertising System

18

I do.
I think.
I feel.

The President's Committee on Employment of the Handicapped
The School of Visual Arts Public Advertising System

19

*Richie Mercado has a good job and his own apartment.
Is this your idea of a retarded person?*

"I only worked a few days my first week," says Richie. "But when I saw that money in my hand I couldn't believe it. I'd never had that much money in my life."

Richie, who is 23, has been working as a jeweler's assistant in Manhattan for 5 years. He spent most of his life in foster homes and state schools for the retarded. Today he shares an apartment in the Bronx with his friend Donald.

Richie and Donald are both part of a program which places retarded adults in apartments throughout the Bronx. Although they are the only retarded people in the building, they get along well with their neighbors.

Richie enjoys his job because he likes working with his hands. There's a new man at work and Richie is teaching him how to stamp rings according to their karats and file them down.

After work Richie sometimes stays in Manhattan to watch a movie. On weekends he sometimes goes fishing off the boats in Sheepshead Bay. "I felt trapped in the state school," says Richie. "Now I'm happy to be free."

President's Committee on Employment of the Handicapped Washington, D.C. 20210 The School of Visual Arts Public Advertising System

20

*"When I speak out for the rights of retarded people,
I know what I'm talking about, because I'm one of them."*

Michael is part of the Association for Children with Retarded Mental Development (A.C.R.M.D.), an organization that fights discrimination against retarded people. He has been their spokesman at many meetings.

Michael has managed to get jobs for a number of retarded people by talking directly to politicians. They call the A.C.R.M.D. and say, "A young man from your organization spoke up and we're interested in hiring someone."

Michael is one of the first retarded people to work full time for the Federal Government. After he was on the job a few years they gave him a special citation for improving the efficiency of the office.

"I had the idea of using a less expensive paper for the office copying machines. It saves the government thousands of dollars a year."

Michael says that the determination of the handicapped of doing a job well and thoroughly is the best argument for hiring them.

President's Committee on Employment of the Handicapped Washington, D.C. 20210 The School of Visual Arts Public Advertising System

21

*"Now it's hard to believe that we had to fight
for Eugene's right to eat lunch with other children."*

"When my son was two and a half, we realized he was retarded," says Harry Kamish. "I was depressed and like most parents in the same situation, completely unprepared to deal with it."

"Although Eugene was allowed to enter school he was hidden away in the 'special class.' The students in this class weren't permitted to go to assembly, gym or lunch with the 'normal' students.

"My wife and I soon realized that we had to fight for our son's rights because there weren't any government agencies that would. We joined with other parents in forming the Association for Children with Retarded Mental Development (A.C.R.M.D.).

"Today Eugene has a full time job. Many things have changed since he was in grade school, but many people still don't realize the potential of retarded people. They get the same satisfaction from doing a job well, if not more, get the same pleasure from relationships, and have the same capacity to give and receive love.

"My son's life is a testimony to this. I'm very proud of him."

President's Committee on Employment of the Handicapped Washington, D.C. 20210 The School of Visual Arts Public Advertising System

"Here I was the first blind graduate of Juilliard and the only job I could get paid $2.25 an hour."

"Most people express horror at the thought of being blind. I'm not knocking 20/20, but I would find it much more difficult not to have the use of my arms, legs or hearing."

When Valerie Capers was six years old she developed a strep throat and the virus settled in her optic nerve leaving her blind. Today she is an associate professor of music at Bronx Community College of the University of the City of New York.

She describes her first year at Juilliard as grueling, particularly at the end of the year performance exams. Each summer she would memorize music so that she could face the beginning of the school year with greater confidence.

After graduation, when she applied for a job teaching music at a neighborhood school, she was asked to audition for the parents. "If I were not blind, I would never have been asked to audition for that kind of job."

About the reaction to disabled people, she says, "people think, 'I'm glad it isn't me.' It arouses their fears and pity. Too often they consider the disabled a drag. They need enlightenment."

If anyone can contribute to that enlightenment, Valerie Capers can. Her zest for her work, her laughter, her professionalism and her impatience to get on with her work make the word "disabled" obsolete.

President's Committee on
Employment of the Handicapped
Washington, D.C. 20210

Produced by The School of Visual Arts Public Advertising System

22

"My eyes are closed, yet somehow without knowing my senses guess what beauty lies between this sunlit nook and those far blue hills."

Those are the words and images of Dr. Robert J. Smithdas, words he hasn't heard and images he hasn't seen since the age of four when he lost his sight and hearing. Dr. Smithdas is a published poet and a member of the American Poetry Society. "I started writing because I like to express myself. That can be said of most writers. And that's how I like to think of myself—just like any other writer."

His own education is a testimony to his strength and the support of others. At the Perkins School for the Blind, he achieved a scholastic average of 97 and dismantled and reassembled the transmission of a Chevrolet engine in 25 minutes. Later at St. John's University, a nonhandicapped student communicated classroom lectures to him through the manual alphabet. A large corps of volunteers transcribed all of his texts into braille. He graduated cum laude with a Bachelor of Arts Degree. Three years later, at New York University, he became the first deaf-blind person to earn a master's degree. In 1975 he married Michelle Craig who is also deaf and blind. He is a Yankee fan, an avid fisherman, a Red Cross swimmer and a man who has been known to tackle the New York subway on his own.

Today, Dr. Smithdas is the Director of Community Education for the Helen Keller National Center for Deaf-Blind Youths and Adults. In this capacity, his own life experience provides a very special sensitivity to the enormous need for rehabilitation of deaf-blind people.

He has proved that with proper rehabilitation, the deaf-blind person can participate fully and successfully in a complex society. He asks that the disabled be treated like any other human beings. Robert Smithdas says it all in his poem "Shared Beauty": "I call it life, and laugh with its delight. Though life itself be out of sound and sight."

President's Committee on
Employment of the Handicapped
Washington, D.C. 20210

Produced by The School of Visual Arts Public Advertising System

23

"When I dance, I feel better and beautiful."

Melissa Berman is nine years old, deaf and a "natural dancer." She takes ballet at the Joffrey Ballet School where Meredith Baylis teaches a special class for the non-hearing. The children respond to the vibration in the floor and sometimes get their instruction through an interpreter.

Dance seems to offer an escape valve for the remarkable energy that would otherwise be bottled up in Melissa and her classmates. Melissa's mother reports that when "The Nutcracker" appeared on television, Melissa got up and joined in the dancing. Melissa is also an accomplished gymnast but her great love is dance which she hopes to pursue.

Here in the dance studio, with the pianist pounding away, Melissa is indeed beautiful!

President's Committee on
Employment of the Handicapped
Washington, D.C. 20210

Produced by The School of Visual Arts Public Advertising System

Photo: David Fullard

24

PROBLEMS 22–24: To show that disabled people are creative members of society.
CLIENT: President's Committee on the Employment of the Handicapped.

PROBLEMS 25–26: To show that the disabled are responsible members of the working community.
CLIENT: President's Committee on the Employment of the Handicapped.

PROBLEMS 27–29: To use personal testimony from the disabled to give the public greater awareness of their humanity.
CLIENT: President's Committee on the Employment of the Handicapped.

Business has never been better
at Marco's Beauty Salon on Second Avenue.

The President's Committee on Employment of the Handicapped
The School of Visual Arts Public Advertising System

25

The parents were angry when she was hired.
Now they're glad she took the job.

The President's Committee on Employment of the Handicapped

26

"When I saw a cripple, I'd stop stark still and walk across the street."

In explaining that reaction, Dr. Colter Rule, a practicing psychiatrist says, "I guess it was a mirror and I was unacceptable to myself."

Dr. Rule was disabled by polio as a child. At five he was sent to an institution that was hundreds of miles from his home. That year away—which he remembers as more like ten years—resulted in a permanent emotional severance from his family. "The way my family responded made me feel it would have been better if I hadn't been born. At the institution, I perfected a superficial charm to get attention and approval. But inside there was an enormous rage that stayed with me for years. As an example of my negativism, when members of my family stressed that it was lucky I could play the piano, since I couldn't dance, that was the last time I touched the piano.

"When I became a doctor I thought, now, I will be dealing with the sick and I won't have to deal with myself. That's why it took me such a long time to identify or get involved with the problems of the disabled."

Dr. Colter Rule sums it up in these words today, "We must work and learn together. After all, an abused child can be more seriously disabled than someone who has difficulty with coordination. We must stop treating any disabled person as a loser and begin to build gateways for them through which they can join the rest of the world."

President's Committee on
Employment of the Handicapped
Washington, D.C. 20210

Produced By The School of Visual Arts Public Advertising System

27

"What's a poor crippled boy from New Jersey doing here?"

"Here" is Hofstra University and Dr. Harold E. Yuker is its provost. "I never dreamed of being a college administrator. I'm the number two person and responsible for a budget of over a million dollars. When the president is away, I run the place."

For a man born with cerebral palsy, it's a long way from an elementary school for crippled children to a top job in a university.

"Long before anyone ever heard of mainstreaming, I wanted to go to a regular high school. After graduating I couldn't get a job anywhere. Luckily, I received a scholarship and earned a degree in Business Administration. Then I earned a Ph.D. in Psychology, and became a teacher. And that's interesting, because I was told many times that I never could be a teacher, because I talked funny and slow. Now I can lecture to 2000 people."

"I believe that there should be practically no institutions that educate only the disabled. The best thing that can happen to disabled people and to the country is for the disabled to be given a chance to compete and interact with everyone else in this world."

"I remember when I was about 11, the guys on the block were challenged to a baseball game. When I was about the 7th person chosen, the opposing captain asked, 'Why did you pick a cripple? Our captain answered, 'I don't think of him as a cripple. He's a lousy baseball player, but you have those on your team too.'"

Harold Yuker might still be the world's worst baseball player, but a lot of people would want him on their team.

President's Committee on
Employment of the Handicapped
Washington, D.C. 20210

Produced By The School of Visual Arts Public Advertising System

28

"I have the same right to live, I want a piece of that same pie and damn it, I'm gonna get it."

Curtis Brewer makes that statement as a lawyer for all the disabled people.

This is a man who has converted anger into a positive force. In 1975 he formed Untapped Resources, the only nonprofit law firm that provides free legal service and counseling exclusively to disabled people. Directly it has helped hundreds of people and indirectly thousands more.

Mr. Brewer is no stranger to obstacles. During his last year of college he developed transverse myelitis and is today a quadriplegic using a wheelchair. However, he finished college on crutches and took the subway to school. In 1974, he graduated from Brooklyn Law School.

"Obstacles," Brewer points out, "come in many sizes, shapes and dispositions. Some can be overcome through hard work and perseverance. But others, that most people never think twice about like stairs, escalators, revolving doors, and public trains, are giant roadblocks to human dignity. These obstacles too often bar the disabled from education, employment and health services."

Curtis Brewer cites the case of a teacher who was afraid that she would lose her job because multiple sclerosis caused her to stumble in the halls. He advised her to tell the truth and he would back her up with a strong letter setting out exactly how the law covered such an eventuality. She's still teaching.

Brewer points out that in grade school, we see John run, but we never see John in a wheelchair. Curtis Brewer is dedicated to changing these patterns. He states with all the authority of someone who's been there. "We don't want sympathy, we want justice. We don't want a hand-out, we want a hand up."

President's Committee on
Employment of the Handicapped
Washington, D.C. 20210

Produced By The School of Visual Arts Public Advertising System

29

217

SOLUTION:

PROBLEM 30: To make rape victims aware of a hot-line counseling service.
CLIENT: New York Women Against Rape.

PROBLEM 31: To promote proper dental hygiene.
CLIENT: New York City Health Department

PROBLEMS 32–33: To encourage rape victims and families to seek help through counseling.
CLIENT: New York Women Against Rape.

PROBLEM 34–35: To make women aware of their rights concerning abortion.

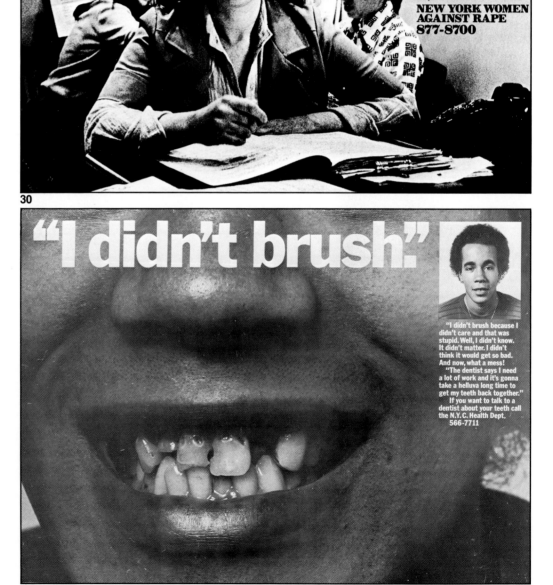

30

31

"I'm 76 years old. I was robbed and raped. By talking with New York Women Against Rape, I didn't have to face it alone."

**Counseling is free and confidential.
(212) 877-8700**

32

"A man raped me on the way home from school. I was afraid to tell my parents. So I got help from New York Women Against Rape."

**Counseling is free and confidential.
(212) 877-8700**

33

"I didn't want to go against my church and my family but I had to. I had to have an abortion.

"It's my life. I'm 17, I'm not married and I wasn't ready to be a mother."

For information on counseling call 354-8688.

The School of Visual Arts Public Advertising System

34

"I had an abortion because I love my family."

"It wasn't an easy decision to make. I mean, I always thought I'd have a big family like my mother's. But when I found out that I was pregnant again, Tom and I knew we weren't ready for another child. I mean, I would have to quit my job and Tom would have to work nights and then he couldn't be with the children much.

"Tom and I want to spend our time with the children now, while they're growing up. And of course we want to make sure they have all they need."

For information on counseling call 354-8688.

The School of Visual Arts Public Advertising System

35

CREDITS

(133)
Masks Poster
Art Director: Richard Wilde
Designer: Diane Addesso
Illustrators: Laura Goodman (Fat Face),
Susan Spivack (BrickFace), Nancy Ward (Bird)
Photographer: Ken Ambrose

(143)
Used Cars for Sale Catalog Cover
Art Directors: Richard Wilde, Bill Kobasz
Designer: Bill Kobasz

(151)
Artifacts Poster
Art Director: Richard Wilde, Skip Sorvino
Designer: Skip Sorvino
Illustrator: Fred Castelluccio

(151)
Artifacts Invitation
Art Director: Richard Wilde
Designer: Skip Sorvino
Illustrator: Paul Cazzolino

(163)
A Matter of Life and Death Poster
Art Director: Richard Wilde
Designers: Bill Kobasz, Susan Spivack
Illustrator: Paul Yalowitz

(169)
Homage to the Palette Poster
Art Director: Richard Wilde
Designers: Ayelet Bender, Diane Addesso
Illustrators: Tom Mennillo, Sean O'Conner,
Issac Kerlow, Michael Grieco, Rita Dubas,
Laura Goodman, Bill Donnelly, and Mark J. Tocchet

(178)
Apartments for Rent Invitation
Art Directors: Richard Wilde, Bill Kobasz
Designers: Bill Kobasz, Kathi Rota
Illustration: Darryl Ligasan

(178)
Apartments for Rent Poster
Art Directors: Richard Wilde, Bill Kobasz
Designers: Bill Kobasz, Kathi Rota
Illustrator: Richard Sierra

(179)
Apartments for Rent Poster
Art Directors: Richard Wilde, Bill Kobasz
Designers: Bill Kobasz, Kathi Rota
Illustrator: Kam Mak

(181)
Extinction Poster
Art Director: Richard Wilde
Designer: Jorge Gonzalez
Illustrator: Joseph Ianelli

(181)
Extinction Button
Art Director: Richard Wilde
Designer: Frank Pastorini
Illustrator: Louis Diaz

(181)
Extinction Advertisement
Art Director: Richard Wilde
Illustrator: Louis Diaz

(185)
Sports: The 21st Century Poster
Art Director: Richard Wilde
Designer: Martha Savitzky
Illustrator: Marc Phelan

(187)
Double Take Poster
Art Director: Richard Wilde
Design: Jorge Gonzalez
Illustrator: Judi Mintzer

(193)
Visual Passages Invitation
Art Director: Richard Wilde
Design: Ayelet Bender
Illustrator: Nancy A. Viglietta

(201)
An Illustration Is Worth A Thousand Words Poster
Art Director: Richard Wilde
Designer: Susan Cullen Eckrote
Illustrator: Roberta Egan

Stained Glass Cieling

Instructors:

Students:

Renee Argule	Diane Kwiecien
Pamela Baderian	Donald Ledwin
John Balkets	Paula Lewis
Arlene Baptiste	Cherry Manning
Stephen Barbara	Michael Marcellino
Katherine Bookas	Jose Martinez
Marsha Boston	JoAnn Messina
Judy Boyle	Jennifer Mitchell
Robert Buggelli	Julian Molesso
Thomas Bunn	Peter Mosen
Leonara Cara	Anne Murray
Amy Chin	Mark Nikkel
James Delapine	Somchai Nontiskul
Donna Diamond	Jeanne Pytlik
Roseanne Di Maio	Rosanne Re
Paula Donis	Ann Marie Renzi
Tina Dunkley	John Ribuffo
Sande Ende	Judith Rice
Warren Fenzi	Eileen Schwartz
Louise Fili	Joan Shafer
Ruth Gallin	Fazl Sherzad
Scott Glaser	Lihi Shye
Janet Gordon	Laurie Sinert
Peter Grannuci	Sandra Skidmore
Richard Grote	Donna Smith
Beth Helfant	Sandra Smith
Muriel Henriques	Debra Sosinsky
Gail Hoffman	Sonja Stadler
Marjorie Impell	Irene Stawicki
Evan Jacobson	Robin Stelzer
Michael Jiminez	Lois Strodl
Thomas Johnson	Stephanie Taddonis
Vernon Jones	Rochelle Trager
William Kalck	Eugene Turner
Nancy Kartanowicz	Anita Lopez Walker
Helen Katchis	Catherine Warnis
Michael Katz	Nevin Washington
Phyllis Kaye	Ann Watt
Lynn Kraut	Sam Woo

Public Advertising System

Instructors:
Frank Young
Regina Ovesey
Richard Wilde

Students:

Nadine Appel	David Pickman
Saul Berger	Joan Reese
Paul Bergwall	Karla Ricciardi
Albert Chiang	Roxanne Salman
Vincent Conti	Lucille Salvia
John DeFrancesco	Ava Sanders
John DeLuca	Joel Sanders
Eric Ennis	Eileen Sandler
Gary Ennis	Joann Scozzafava
Ivan Fernandes	Mark Segall
Meredith Field	Allison Seifer
Susan Fineman	Daphne Shuttleworth
David Fullard	Fred Slavin
Lauren Giber	Dan Soldan
Robert Goldstein	Darrel Spencer
Laura Goodman	Steve Toriello
Mario Guia	Nicholas Verni
Denise Halpin	Stephanie Wicks
Barbara Hamilton	Anne Winslow
Deborah Hyde	Alan Zindman
Rosemary Intrieri	
George Kontaxis	
Sheila Kotkin	
Wayne Krush	
Tony Labozzetta	
Dane Lachiusa	
Steven Lansberg	
John Lei	
Vicki Levites	
Calvin Lowery	
Stewart Martin	
Deborah Mattison	
Robert Mizrahi	
Mary Moran	
Kirk Mosel	
Mark Nussbaum	
Ronald Palumbo	
Steven Parenti	
Joanne Pateman	

PROBLEM ACKNOWLEDGEMENTS

Part 1. All the problems in Part 1 were created by Richard Wilde with the exception of the Head and Body problem, which was created by Marshall Arisman. Also, the Heart Plus the Letter *H* problem is a variation of a problem given by Armin Hofmann at the Basil School of Design, Switzerland.

Part 2. All the problems in Part 2 were created by Richard Wilde and Marshall Arisman with the exception of the Matter of Life and Death problem, which was originated by Carl Titolo. Leo and Diane Dillon were responsible for the Stained-glass Ceiling project. Thanks to all the instructors of the School of Visual Arts whose students participated in the exhibitions, with a special thanks to Jack Endewelt, the late Gilbert Stone, Leo and Diane Dillon, Adrienne Leban, Frank Young, Skip Sorvino, Russ D'Anna, Carlos Llerena, Patti Bellantoni, Sam Martine, Carl Titolo, and Robert Weaver.

Part 3. All the problems in Part 3 were coordinated by Richard Wilde. Frank Young and Regina Ovesey were responsible for the Public Advertising System.

INDEX